Fishing Without Tears

Match Fishing

Fishing Without Tears

WILLIAM HILL

Pelham Books

First published in Great Britain by
PELHAM BOOKS LTD
52 Bedford Square
London, W.C.1
1973

© 1973 by William Hill

All Rights Reserved. No part of this publication
may be reproduced, stored in a retrieval system,
or transmitted, in any form or by any means,
electronic, mechanical, photocopying, recording or
otherwise, without the prior permission of the
Copyright owner

ISBN 7207 0649 1

Set and printed in Great Britain by
Tonbridge Printers Ltd
Peach Hall Works, Tonbridge, Kent
in Caledonia eleven on twelve point
on paper supplied by P. F. Bingham Ltd
and bound by Dorstel Press, Harlow

For Donald Fletcher, who first
put a rod in my hand – and with
sympathy for those who are boys now.

Contents

	Preface	11
1.	Lonely Guardian	13
2.	A Bit Behind the Times	18
3.	Moments of Triumph	22
4.	The Rod To Beat Them With	26
5.	'My Chub Hooks, Bill!'	29
6.	The Master Method	34
7.	The Ultimate Art	38
8.	It's In the Bin	43
9.	Success is Relative	48
10.	Right! Let's 'Ave You...	52
11.	The Grand Return	57
12.	Dry Line In Deutschland	61
13.	In Time of Flood	68
14.	Once, They Never Were...	72
15.	Women and Fishing	78
16.	The Fact About Digby	82
17.	What Is It... A Sprat?	87
18.	Walton's Walk	93
19.	One In The Eye With A Wet Myth	98
20.	On The Other Side	103
21.	Monster in Weak Tea	108
22.	Of Charms and Fancies	113
23.	Beauty – I Tell You It's Torture!	117
24.	Something For the Wall	121
25.	It Was Something Big!	126
26.	Secret Stronghold	132
27.	Long-Lost Christmas	136
28.	Last Cast	141

Illustrations

Line Drawings

Frontispiece (Match Fishing)	2
Lonely Guardian	14
Ultimate Art	39
Success is Relative	49
The Grand Return	58
Dry Line in Deutschland	62
Women and Fishing	79
The Wet Myth	99
Of Charms and Fancies	114
Something Big...	127
Long-Lost Christmas	137

Photographs
  (*Between pages* 64 *and* 65)
1. One Man Bought the View to go with his Fishing
2. The Author
3. The Red Dustbin
4. Women and Fishing
5. Contrast to 'Monster in Weak Tea'
6. ... Of Charms and Fancies?
7. Not the 'Secret Stronghold'
8. Home Stream

Drawings by Anne Hill

Preface

While some of the bits and pieces in this book were appearing in *Angling* – they are reproduced here by kind permission of the Editor – I had one letter from a man who had never been fishing in his life. He picked up the magazine by accident and wrote to say that he understood exactly what I was getting at, but was sad that an awful lot of people wouldn't believe it.

Well, I suppose anglers write about fishing because it's the best way of filling in time before going fishing – but there's a new and more urgent reason creeping in. Perhaps this is a sense of time being short.

But my correspondent had a point. Even if you play it for laughs, most people don't want to be bothered by the End of the World. And those who do can read more about it in the last chapter of this book.

W.H.

1. Lonely Guardian
   (from *Angling*, December 1967)

I saw him glowing in the distance, and just went on fishing. It was a good day, and difficult fishing, but perhaps I should have been more alert. For suddenly I got words battering at me from behind.

'Here! Whatta you doing?' shouted the man with the red neck.

'You can't fish here,' he said, coming up fast and with the side of his red neck throbbing.

'Why?' I asked.

'Because this is the club stretch, that's why.'

Now, not being able to fish in a particular place is one of life's more unpleasant experiences. And it can, of course, be one of life's more dangerous experiences. This looked dangerous.

He had changed from a casual waterside walker with a mongrel dog, to a vigilante snorting in righteous rage. While the vein in his neck was working away I thought of that bright little saying that goes something like: you can kick a man's wife, but just try kicking his dog and see what happens.

This, unfortunately, goes farther where anglers are concerned. You can kick a man's dog, but if you cast half a breadcrumb on his water or wave half a rod tip over his rushes, then look out.

It wasn't as if I'd been doing some classic poaching for profit. Behind me was no London gang with tins of poison. And I was not in the position of a man who has sneaked a coach-full of anglers to the Test in the hope that they can fish an all-in match without anyone noticing.

Lonely Guardian

In this case I had barely a foot (well, perhaps two) on the wrong side of a notice board. It didn't quite justify all the menace, outrage and rancour built into that 'You can't fish here!'

I was in fact trying out for a first season some salmon water which gurgled invitingly round a moderately famous name and looked – awful. The trouble was that it could be described as cheap fishing, a cheapness justified by the fact that all that beautiful chalk stream was approachable in only three places. All the rest twinkled between banks that were either jungle, and completely man-proof, or bog that sucked the waders off you in one satisfied slurp.

With a good rod and only small experience, anyone could cast the whole length of my cheap bit of salmon water. What's more, I could only fish it on one day a week. A day in the middle of the week, too. My friends didn't envy me.

For these reasons I looked longingly at the other side of the notice board. On that side some miracle had taken place. The banks were firm there and the trees and bushes behaved like gentlemen. So I just took one pace to the right,

stepped over a temptingly low fence and was fishing happily
– pushing the Allcock Yellow Belly across and down without
a worry in my mind.

When the man came up I was taking some weed off the
treble. Inside, I cowered a bit. But outside, I looked just
faintly surprised, as if I hadn't noticed where I was.

I've never seen this work.

Lots of people do it when caught in embarrassing situations, and lots of people fail. The power goes to those who
know they are in the right, and the power ebbs from those
who know they are in the wrong.

Staring bravely at the angry man I said I was sorry. Then
I did a braver thing. Resisting the urge to hook my Yellow
Belly's treble in his ear, I made a final, forbidden cast. I
fished it out... slowly... in front of his face.

It was a tense moment. He was so worked up that he
looked more energetic than a gorilla in the mating season,
and more fierce than a motorist who has just had his boot
crushed in.

In all my life I have never enjoyed a cast less. For a long
second I had the impression that he was about to do something really primitive – like knocking my hat off. But he
didn't.

After stepping one pace to the left and getting safely back
on my side of the notice board, I was able to ignore him in
good conscience, though he stood for some time waving his
arms and spluttering about being an 'ex officio bailiff' of
so and so's club.

Then I actually had a hefty take from something or other
(it turned out to be a small pike) which seemed like a reward
for going back to the straight and narrow path – even if it
did happen to be a path covered in bog and brambles.

The plain fact is that you can't enjoy your fishing if you
must be forever looking over your shoulder. I know one or
two fishermen who think a bit of trespass adds spice to life,
but my feeling is that they do it because straightforward
legal fishing has lost some of its savour. This is sad, very
sad.

Such poaching is like an endless quest to satisfy the jaded
palate, and bound to fail. Yet even those who don't practise
poaching to any marked degree must still chafe at restric-

tions and feel that trespass isn't morally wrong. Which of us doesn't feel it is somehow immoral that there should be other men's fishing? That this bank is ours and that is theirs? That here we can fish on certain days, and there we can never fish?

We need licences and tickets or influence, as much as we need reels and hooks and time off. Once, the old men tell me, it wasn't like that. And it wasn't.

Things are so changed that the time of freedom seems like a dream. For we anglers in the second half of the 20th Century fishing is divided into sections marked by notice boards and barbed wire. We move like chessmen from square to square and, when coming upon that interesting little stream that wanders off on its own, we must fuss over permissions and payments.

Whatever happens in the future this situation is not going to improve. It can only get worse. This is why I can reveal my real feelings towards that spluttering man who wanted to kick me off his water. At the time I resented him as I resent all the restrictions upon our angling freedom. At the time I thought him ridiculous and funny. In the calm afterwards I knew he was right. I see him now as a lonely man, standing out against the tragedy of our times.

Some say 'tragedy' is far too strong a word for describing the effects of overpopulation. But there are too many bodies on too small an island. The result is destruction of the things we love and need. This is tragedy.

We kill through what has been so aptly called our 'terrible fecundity'. As each new soul opens its eyes upon its heritage an acre disappears and a tree falls. As population pressure builds up it brings neuroses, and thousands of acres are churned away for ever.

The land is dying. Beauty is dying. Going out with a rod is no longer merely a quiet retreat; it is now a scurry towards sanity, an attempt to grasp at fading health. For a few short hours you want to walk without having to dodge others who walk against you and around you.

Underneath... the earth. Overhead... the sky. Before you the world of water and fish – clean, unsullied, yours. This is the desire. More often than not it is an illusion, because you aren't alone. It is not just other anglers who are with you, but the breath and works of 55 millions.

Once-bright rivers are now rushing down pipes, 'Living Units' sit upon the water's edge and in all the air lives the noise of battling vehicles. Across the fields as you pass the pylons walk with wire on their shoulders. Underneath them is paper, tin and plastic excreted from an age living on dross.

One of my wealthier acquaintances has built himself a shield against the situation. He has bought not only his own stretch of trout stream, but also the view to go with it. The cost was high but he has now secured a bit of Fishing England and will preserve it against the multitude. No doubt he will put up notice boards; so would I in his place. But I am not wealthy.

I think my 'ex officio bailiff' wasn't a wealthy man either. I also think that, subconsciously, he felt the pressures about him without rationalising them. In a sense he was saying to me: 'By banding together in a club, with a limited number of people, I have gained breathing space. This is *my* river. *My* ground. I dare not let you in because you are millions and will destroy the thing I love'.

2. A Bit Behind the Times
(from *Angling* October 1967)

A lot of people take heart from the feeling that the dizzily spinning everyday world of work and worry has not yet got its nervous fingers on the ancient craft of angling. As a matter of fact, they know that angling is an antidote to false values.
 I know this too, but with a difference. I am vigilant. More than that – I am prepared to go extremes in order to guard against this invasion. That is why I do not own a rod built of glass, and why I shall never own one. And that goes for rods built of steel, too.
 If anyone thinks there's precious little connection between the pattern of society and glass or steel rods, then he may be right. The only thing is, I think he's been got at.
 Once I saw some photographs of Americans fishing in a deluxe manner from pontoons – centrally-heated pontoons enclosed by glass and with a hole through which their rods poked. By their sides were – not a bait tin or a bag of groundbait – but cocktails! They had been got at too. That's how far it can go.
 Mind you, I'm not saying that anybody who buys a glass rod is only one step away from being an automaton. I don't even have very much against glass rods as rods. Those I have handled did feel a little odd (one even made a cracking sound at the butt end) yet I have no evidence that they are inadequate for the jobs they are designed to do. And I am not suggesting that the day is close when you will throw away your glass rod after each fishing expedition like a disposable paper plate.
 What I shudder at is the material itself. I think glass and

steel are subversive, even unnatural, when you consider the nature of angling. Progressively minded fishermen know in their bones that this is a lot of small-minded claptrap. Some I know even think it is worse. They say it is reactionary die-hardism, which sounds very nice, but is meant to be a roundabout way of saying something very nasty.

'Do you want us to go back to whalebone tips and horsehair lines?' they say. And they say it in such a way as to imply that I am a simple lad who prefers to believe that pike really do spring, fully toothed, from the womb of water weed.

Well, I don't believe that. I'd rather like to believe it, though, just as I think it would be rather pleasant to know that pike will not eat tench because old shovel tail really is a doctor fish, who might be needed one day when they come up against bigger pike.

These days we all know a lot of useful things. We are all becoming very knowledgeable indeed. Very efficient too. I'd like to think that this awareness gives us a lot more to wonder at, but it doesn't seem to work that way.

It is not a question of being against all the improvements that have steadily come upon angling through the centuries. On a mantlepiece somewhere I have an old brass reel which has scarcely the diameter of a crown piece. An old man gave it to me and I polished it so that the worn and pitted brass glowed. The old man said his grandfather had done the same thing. I suppose I keep this reel as a sort of ornament. Certainly I'd never dream of using it; the rate of retrieve must be agonisingly slow and the line capacity quite laughable.

My own centrepins are big and made of some sort of alloy. They spin fast as a breath and can be controlled by finger and thumb. They also give my critics a chance to pounce. 'I suppose you call your alloy reels natural,' they say. No, I don't. They are no more or less natural than a glass or steel rod – or manufactured and glued cane, come to that. It is all a matter of drawing the line somewhere and, sadly, that's a pun that attracts even less interest than the idea behind it.

I accept fixed-spool reels, for instance, though confessing to some fellow-feeling for those who pilloried the early threadliners as devils who would remove every fish in the river within half an hour. My own fixed-spool reel is something I would never be without. I have learned to forget that I saw where it was made. In fact, it was not so much made as compiled.

There was no single person involved. No one you could point out as having made my reel. At a rough guess I'd say that it came to me through the disinterested efforts of at least five young girls. In the factory I saw them chattering along the conveyor belt, deftly handling the component parts while thinking of boy friends, what Mrs So-and-So said during the tea break, and a new shade of hair tint.

I also accept other things. Nylon, for instance (wasn't gut ghastly when you look back?) is a godsend too. In fact I consider that I am being extremely reasonable about it all. However, though I am a modern angler I take no pride in being one. There's no such thing as a modern fish, or a modern tree – even if the fish was tipped from a water-filled dustbin in a re-stocking programme, and the tree was transplanted from 20 miles away.

Sometimes I think there are large numbers of anglers whose days of fishing seem more like mechanical handling exhibitions. The synthetic capture of a wild creature is an uncomfortable thought.

Rods, though, are so basically necessary, so much angling's insignia, that artificiality jars me to the marrow. Put it simply: does anyone get the same pleasure from buying a glass rod as from buying a cane one? Buying a rod is a great occasion, long thought about beforehand.

Recently I spent a whole hour deciding on a rod. It seemed a very short hour to me and like a day to the shopkeeper, but what did I care if he tapped his toes and looked as if he wanted to go to the lavatory. For him there was a delay of the sale; for me there was the even-baked splendour of the cane to discover, the quality of varnish, the almost sensual feel of its balance in the hand. Show me the man who gets the same pleasure from fibre glass or alien steel.

It seems to me that most of us like to think our possessions have been built by craftsmen. Some deluded souls even buy motor cars after convincing themselves that this or that mass production unit produces better workmanship. No one thinks of his car as being just another frail bubble of coloured tin, stuck about with plastic and chromium plate.

My car doesn't interest me much, which is probably why I can condemn them all so heartily. But my rods do interest me, particularly those which I have seen made. They came from a place which is out of this century.

I found the factory in two dark sheds lost in back streets. There was dust under the roof and over the floor, and an apprentice in spectacles beside a treadle lathe. He looked ready to call his boss 'master' and master looked ready to despatch his apprentice for a pannikin of good ale and some hot dumplings wrapped in a red spotted handkerchief.

The rodmakers spoke lovingly of cane 'temperament', and were happy to disappear and reappear between sheaves of cane and gluepots with examples of good and bad. I knew that they were up to their top joints in orders. No wonder they didn't hurry. If they did they wouldn't be.

I have never seen those who make the other types of rods. But I have seen fibre glass boats made. It was all clean and quick, white coats slapping on layers of what looked like coarse wire wool. The stuff made the fingers itch and the lungs feel hard. Making rods of modern materials may be high science; I doubt if it is high art.

There is satisfaction in having to varnish your rod every second year or so. Satisfaction, too, in the way they nod to the fish. Wood bends to the power of flesh and fin and has an affinity with it.

Maybe there is some other strange happiness for those whose rods were at some stage spun by white-coated spiders or drawn at white heat from a fire and tempered with angry hissings. Anglers who are content with such devices are probably well-adjusted modern men.

Nobody can walk out from his society, but I prefer to leave one foot, and my rods, just a little way behind.

3. Moments of Triumph

I want to announce that I have just finished making a float. The design came from an old fishing magazine and, to tell the truth, I'm rather proud. I think it is a great achievement ... not quite on the level of the Venus space probe perhaps, or that tunnel they dug through the Alps, but something quite exceptional for me.

The art of making things has always been given to other people. Say what you like about the creative delights and I'll agree. Mention the economics of the matter and I'll agree more. But I still shudder at Do-It-Yourself, and wince when passing those shops that have ladders and bits of hardboard outside.

So this float is a big event, which is why I now have it lying on its side so that the light twinkles on its superb lines and paintwork. Something I knocked up myself, this. Just a little something.

The designer's instructions were encouraging, and as I happened to be looking for a satisfactory grayling float (those I had used for years seemed to be letting me down a bit) I cleared the room, spread yards of newspaper all over it, assembled enough tools to build an office block... and started. The magazine told me that any reasonably handy chap could produce the float in half an hour, and I believed it. A week later, I won through. Standing on a pile of balsa shavings and an overturned paint pot, I said 'Eureka' (actually, I think it was 'Thank God that's over!') and waved the float aloft in one bandaged hand. It is amazing what a razor blade can do when it snaps.

The painting I rather liked. I went all patriotic in red,

white and blue. As a matter of fact it was more cunning than that as, reading from tip down, it was red, blue and white.

Why the white on the lower, or underwater section? Scientific anglers say the latest theory is that white is probably what the sky looks like from fishdom, and as the sky is invisible... well, it's something like that anyway.

The blue colour went in because it was all I had to separate the white from the red. And of course I had red on top because who would dream of having anything else? Oh, I know about fluorescence and how good black is for a float tip, in certain conditions of light. But nothing would have made me top off my creation in black.

My float is worth going on about because it is significant. The last time I took up tools was when I was around eleven years old, which is a frightful long time before DIY came into the language. In fact it was back in the days when even a 'handyman' was not a bank clerk running around the attic in overalls, but a little man who sawed large logs or built you a dog kennel, all for sixpence and a cup of tea.

On that far-off occasion, the middle joint of my whole-cane boy's rod snapped off above the ferrule. It snapped because of a pike – which is a more interesting cause than old age and cheap cane.

This, I remember, was a rush job. Next day I was due to go fishing, and when you are eleven the next fishing trip is the goal of all existence.

The only tackle dealer for miles around didn't have a ferrule of the right size, though perhaps he didn't look for long enough in his cardboard box of jumbled odds and ends. I know he kept asking me if I wanted a male or a female one or both and I didn't understand. Still, being quite a knowledgeable lad I may have guessed what he was driving at and didn't believe it. Anyway, I felt embarrassed.

An iron fact faced me. A broken rod. No ferrule. It still faced me when all the shops were closed and fishing was only a short bedtime away.

Panic set in. I gave up fiddling with the family saw which had been rusting away in the toolshed for years. I threw away the rasp which had taken all the mottling off the cheap cane without in the least cleaning up the broken end – and I rushed, hot and furious and alarmed, to the home of the friend who was to fish with me in the morning.

It was a tremendous blow in the vitals to see his tackle already packed and his rod – it was a new one, a birthday present – standing intact and shining, ready to catch fish of its own accord.

His face blackened in sympathy at the horror of it all. No greater evil had ever come upon me and he understood it. Then he thought a little and took me off to the garage. There was no rod to lend me, but his father's father had fished once and there were some bits and pieces lying around.

We rummaged among the cobwebs in dark corners. The mahogany butt-end of an ancient sea rod emerged from the spidery shadows behind an old gramophone, and was thrown aside. We dived in again. Under a mouse cage, long unused, was a broken landing net handle bound to a blackened wood reel by brittle line that puffed into fragments. My friend looked at it and said he didn't know that was there – and got lost in a lot of tinkering with the reel.

I plunged onward. It was getting dark outside the garage window.

Finally I found a middle joint. It was twice as long as my broken one and only fitted the rest of my rod with the help of cardboard stuffed into the ferrules. But I had a complete rod ... sagging heavily, but complete. 'That'll do' my friend said carelessly, in the way a shy hero might act after saving me from drowning in the weir.

I don't say I am able to measure out my life in triumphs, but finding that floppy old middle joint in that dark garage is certainly one of them. Finding that, with a bit of effort and a penknife, it could be made to fit, is certainly another.

No memory comes to me of whether I caught anything after the triumph, but I like to think I did. That middle joint served me well for another three years, by which time I had grown old enough to despise it.

Looking at my new handmade float now, though, does revive that old satisfaction. When I use it the movement is sure and clean, its behaviour in wind and under line-drag is masterly.

There's something of eager youth to be gained as it sails away down river – even if now I can cast it with any one of seven rods and none is broken.

4. The Rod to Beat Them With

The other day I saw a newspaper report of a fishing competition which read like an uneasy mixture of cut-throat football and anti-Commie jungle war. Notice, too, that I say fishing competition, not 'GRAND SLAM AMONG FIGHTING REDFINS,' or even 'HOT RODS FLAY BOMB BLASTERS IN TOP TEAM NEEDLE BLITZ.'

I thought of that when I was seeing a man about a Rod. He was chuffed; I was chuffed – and I have a cut finger to prove it. And, as well as the cut finger, I have powdered brass in my scalp and hands. That's to prove the contrast between giddy expertise and the sense of wonder – frantic pressure fishing and something once called peaceful enjoyment.

The Rod is responsible for all this. It makes you pause and think. The Rod is so valuable I'm thinking of putting subdued lighting around it and charging 5 pence a look.

Quite possibly it's the heaviest, ugliest, cheapest and most useless thing of value I've ever handled. Except that one day I'm going to win a fishing competition with it.

The brass I keep finding in odd corners of my body comes from an evening spent doing things with electric sanders and ferrules which should only be done by extremely silly or extremely agile men. But it's all in honour of the Rod. And it's all worth it. Ask Bill in the tackle shop.

I found this shop after a lifetime's search (see elsewhere in this book) and now Bill knows I collect old rods at low prices which people have traded-in. Cane, cane, all the way ... and don't put glass anywhere in my sight even though you say it's more efficient, which it usually is.

The Rod to Beat Them With

'Bought this one for half a crown' I said lightly. In spoken English I do try to forget decimals.

Bill handled the Rod like it had dropped off a table at Sotheby's.

'Ah' he said. 'Ah... hum'. Then he said: 'This is very interesting'.

Before him, lying beside something from Hardy and something from Farlows, The Rod looked like a kind of Walkerian nightmare.

But we doted on its specifications. Lancewood top, mottled cane butt and middle, black hardwood handle. The cunning simplicity of too few snake rings, so that you know all about rainy days when trotting; the supreme disregard for balance or action or test curves or tapers. Exotic!

Bill said I wasn't going to believe this, but he knew the firm who made it, and sold it to Gamages. He knew because he started work there in the dear dead days. Then he put on his glasses and studied the stamp on the thin brass butt fittings which were placed so low down as to make reeling-in an effort of willpower and hard training.

'And I remember the man who did the stamping', Bill said. It was my turn to say 'Ah' with meaning, poetry and respect.

The Rod is the forerunner of those which angling experts warn beginners about. But in 1925 someone saved five bob for it and loved it deeply.

Around that time, the firm who made the Rod were producing something like 250,000 poles of all types each year. That's when experts who didn't warn boys about mottled cane and lancewood, probably warned about two pieces of furrulless bamboo with one wire tip ring and nothing else. The price of those, according to Bill's memory, was around 1s 9d for two dozen.

But I'm sure that when the Rod was new it had its place in the tackle cupboards of men who gave advice. No doubt many a bream-bashing needle match was won with it – only the proud angler said he'd been fishing with some blokes and didn't need a tranquilliser in order to unwind afterwards.

The man who stamped names and numbers on the Rod was big and powerful and always wore a white overall with snuff down the front.

The person who put the mottling on the whole-cane was a 16-year-old apprentice who spent days over a gas jet. But he was a cut above other mottler apprentices because they hadn't graduated to the sort of mottling on the Rod, which is circular and not streaky. Streaky was easy: circular was art.

My refitting work – the whipping, sticking, snake-ringing and varnishing – has been true pleasure. Apart from that grayling float I don't usually find the ability to tinker with tackle. Re-ferrulling hasn't been so easy (they were all bastard sizes in the original, and tapered with it) but the result is satisfying.

I have put the Rod in the rack, flanked on one side by my James 'Avocet' and on the other by a preserved Allcocks 'Gunner' sea trouter. A handy construction from Sealey nods at it and a Sharpes 'Carp' looks as if it doesn't notice.

But the Rod is what it is all about. It stands for a simpler, easier time when money was shorter and fishing broader.

I shall fish with it in the next club competition. Think of the symbolism if I win! Think of the triumph! All the top anglers – and we have a few in my club I can tell you – utterly confounded and slinking away with their glass tucked between their legs.

But I hope I don't get stuck into a barbel or something. I have grave doubts about those new ferrules.

5. 'My Chub Hooks, Bill!'
(from *Angling*, March 1968)

Nobody has ever worked it out, but when it comes to wise words there must be more written and spoken on the subject of angling than on any other sport or pastime.

On the river bank the wise words are likely to be short and to the point.

Like a gruff: 'You should be fishing twenty feet farther out,' or an even more demoralising: 'You won't catch anything there.'

All the same, it seems to me that advice at the waterside is usually given with a certain humility and, as a result, is accepted with a certain grace. This is because both adviser and advised are face to face, and the effects of advice are quite likely to show pretty rapidly – for good or ill.

It is different with written wisdom. The best wise words may be filed away in print, though there are so many that you would be hard put to pick out the wisest, if asked to do so straight away. And when there's a rod in your hand wisdom is wanted instantly, just like that.

If I had to pick out the difference between written and spoken wisdom I'd say that the latter rarely leads to a blazing row. The former can cause the most contemplative of men to choke and writhe, bang his fist on the table... and reach for *his* writing paper.

Controversy comes so easily in angling. Mr Blenks-Parr publishes an article about greased-line fishing for salmon and declares, with a blink at the vastness and sacred nature of the subject, that the grease used should be candle tallow and nothing else will do (his reasons fill a full two pages).

He also declares that the fly should be sunk exactly 1.5 millimetres below the ripple, and no more.

This sets the ulcers prodding and causes such a flare of hatred that you might think we were changing the pound to the dollar tomorrow morning. Is Mr Blenks-Parr a thundering nitwit? they say in letters which scorch the editor's table. Anybody caught using such ludicrous and ham-fisted methods on their rivers deserves all he gets!

Somebody else jumps in with a different body blow, and recalls that old Jock McGilgaff has been using tallow for years and though he doesn't know much about millimetres, always calculates the depth of the fly's immersion by the thickness of his slimy thumbnail.

In other places where as much wisdom is given, only more often, the angling giants whose names are engraved on the rods of lesser men come out with homelier but no less profound statements.

'Whatever you do, wear felt slippers when you fish'... and 'Don't clomp around the bank in wellingtons,' says one. Fine. Fair enough. Except that this draws a hoot and a snarl from the last captor of a two-pound roach whose foot size is 13 and never a handicap even when encased in a mountain of welded rubber.

'Stain your nylon yellow with green spots when carp fishing,' says another. Derision from a crack Northerner who says stuff that for a game of anglers, everybody knows that simple tea-staining is good enough.

Well, I know the arguments are often more complex, even sensible. But the sad fact is that anybody who communicates his wisdom about the gentle craft to his gentle brothers lays himself open to a counter-fire of wisdom violently opposed to his own.

It is the security of print that does the trick. I have never seen a duel in the flesh which even remotely approaches the written ones. A short jab or two in the pub usually ends with a 'Get away!' or a 'Never!' or a 'Not so, old boy!' ...and an amicable pint calms everything down. The giants with many truths dripping from their pens appear not as benefactors but as men we love to hate. They stand up boldly to get their heads chopped off.

Few people are grateful to these sages – unless it is gratitude for the chance to chop – but I am grateful to one of them who, as far as I know, has never written down his wisdom.

Early in my fishing career, when things were bright and new and more perplexing than they have ever seemed since, I was sucking in advice as avidly as ever a great club-headed chub gulped cheese. And it was chub and cheese that made the wise man tap me on the shoulder.

I was buying some legers, the first of many I was later to hurl into a fast river that runs under an old stone bridge. Before me, on the tackle dealer's counter, was a large box filled with bullets, anti-kink vanes, split shot, coffin leads, spiral leads, plummets etc. I had been shuffling through them for some time, thinking about current and chub, when that tap on the shoulder came.

'Chub, is it?' said the man behind the tap.

'Yes,' I said, selecting some solid-looking Arlesey bombs which were weighed in my mind and my hand as being most likely to hold bottom in the fast heavy water.

'Too heavy,' he said, pulling in his breath with a tut and a smile. 'You don't want those things'.

I recognised him as one of the shopkeepers in the little town. He knows everybody and chats with everybody, and often he stops beside you on the river bank while taking his dog for a walk.

'Now you take my advice, you want some of these,' he said, dipping into the compartments of the dealer's box, and pulling out a number of little leaden cylinders that you could almost blow away with a puff.

I must have looked uncommonly stupid because he went on to take complete charge.

'Bill!' he called. 'My chub hooks, Bill.'

Bill the tackle dealer, moved quickly (almost as if he knew the routine) and produced another box, this time crammed with hooks. Whereupon my wise helper thrust his hand into the spiky mass and brought out some huge and wickedly barbed hooks with offset points. They were really immense, and seemed more suitable for tying to rope and climbing cliffs.

'You stop your lead about a foot from the hook. Get a lump of cheese, and I mean a good lump ... big as a golf ball... and mould it well round... like this...

He moulded away in mid-air. 'I know about chub, he'll tell you – won't you Bill? He knows what I can do with the old chub.'

Bill nodded. I said... 'Er... um... what about the current, rather fast here isn't it?' The wise man smiled and sighed.

'Listen, old son, that's what they all say when they first come here. Take no notice. You don't want it to hold bottom.

'Use a good springy rod and cast across the stream. Let the current bring the lead round like this...' He adopted the wise chub catcher's stance, and we could almost see the rod in his hand.

'They wait in the current, watching, watching for food'. He whispered dramatically, extending his fingers in the air and making a shoal of chub. 'Then they move to take... bump... bump... bump, you can feel the lead coming across the weed. Then there's a pluck... LIKE THAT! (tapping me on the wristwatch). Tap, tap and... ah... you give a little line and draw back and... HE'S ON!'

It was good advice I can tell you. Practical advice. And so well delivered that there seemed to be no need to be among real tugging and plucking chub.

Not that rolling cheese for chub is anything new. Experienced anglers all know about it, or should anyway. But until that wise man tapped and told me, with all the skill of a folk-lore monger round the tribal fire, it was a method that had never come alive to me.

Later I found it was as he said. There is a certain place on the outside of a bend where the rushes grow high. Here I discovered I could conjure chub almost at will.

No. I go further. I can get chub at will and no 'almost' about it. Chub and cheese is now my top ego booster. Only the other evening I had ten hefty fellows from the spot and got tired of catching them. It made me remember the advice of years ago. They all pluck plucked after the bump bumping.

On second thoughts, I back down. I withdraw the implication that I can guarantee chub. Guarantees are no part of angling wisdom. I'll just say that I always pat that man's dog, and the other day I gave his master a whole tin of maggots when the bait shop was closed and he wanted to snatch an hour away from his counter.

Practical return for practical advice.

6. The Master Method

Of all the failings that prevent you from becoming the complete master of angling craft, I would guess that bowing down before a method is the most stupid and the most deadly. It is bad enough to have a favourite swim which is not only a favourite but the only place on the water where you feel happy. It is even worse to believe absolutely and utterly in one sort of bait. And the height of foolishness is to be so trapped by gadgetry that you think only more gadgets will bring success. But to place complete faith in a certain style of fishing, particularly when that style has a gadget attached, means disaster sooner or later.

Unfortunately it often seems that the disasters come later. Much later, after you have been lured on so far that they don't seem like disasters, but merely bad luck. And, as we all know, luck is not only unimportant... it is something you must ignore.

Someone said somewhere that the man who takes his stand entirely on luck deserves to get only what luck brings, and that is going to be very little. It is equally true that the man who takes his stand entirely on one type of fishing method will succeed only when that method is right... and fail every other time.

I suppose that, ideally, a method is right when it suits water conditions, temperature, the swim situation, the balance of tackle used, the bait, the time of year and even, no doubt, the physical capabilities of the angler. To hit upon all these, or even a large number of them, at the same time, is something you would not put money on. Better not to gamble then; better by far to adapt the method to the conditions, not to cross your fingers and hope the conditions will somehow magically adapt to the method.

Some men have the angler's equivalent of green fingers (slimy fingers?) and never bow down before a method. But they are the giants of the specimen records. They are the experts who, finding that the wife needs a new washing machine, pick up their rods, go out to the matches, and quickly knock up the cash.

Such men exist, but they are rare. I have only known one, or perhaps two, who could be certain to catch fish under any conditions. They did it by watercraft and the correct use of knowledge, rather than by any particular method used for its own sake.

On the last occasion I saw such mastery we were at the back end of the coarse fishing season and most of us returning fishless from the river in the cold. We found our expert with his net full of the most delicious roach and dace... fully twelve or thirteen pounds there were. Not one roach was under the half-pound mark and two were rubbing their snub noses against the two-pound mark. The dace were equally fine and fat.

How did he do it? Well... while the snow lay on the bank he pondered, scratched his head, did a bit of remembering. Then he used a chrysalis. On a tiny hook. In the shallows. Amazing. On our river and at that time nobody I know would have thought of doing that. In high summer, yes. In deep winter, no.

But it worked. And it wasn't luck. The expert was working to a careful, skilful plan based on experience. Most of us would have trotted down deep in the river, or legered an eddy, or rolled the cheese. Most of us did. Most of us failed to catch fish.

Of course it is important that you recognise a master and learn from the right people. I think I am wiser now, but once I wasn't and it hurt. That was when I thought I had found a master. Walton had nothing on him. I was convinced that he had discovered The Method. If anything, it was even worse than that; something to shudder at, blush over.

No sooner had I met the master I became unworthily anxious in case somebody else had. I didn't want anyone else to meet him until I had time to burst forth upon my local angling world with the new knowledge.

The new knowledge, the master's method, my secret was ... the Swim-Feeder.

By now there can be few coarse fishermen who have never heard of the swim-feeder – that small cylinder of perforated perspex weighted along its length by a narrow strip of lead. But in those days it was new.

The feeder was originally designed to be used with a cumbersome form of tackle. This came in a cardboard box as a complete outfit and included a float like a pike bung. No one, I am sure, has ever used it like this, as a float fishing method.

But the quiet man sitting in the early morning mist under river trees in Sussex was legering with the swim-feeder. He was, I understood, the originator of the method. The method, I understood, always worked if you knew what you were doing.

I watched him take great flopping dustbin-loads of bream from the Arun. There were dace too and hordes of solid, fighting roach. It was something to marvel at. I marvelled.

He was casting across the curve of the river which ran steadily with the rains of January and dropping his tackle under the opposite bank where it swung round in an arc before coming to rest. Then, when each cast was made, his two-piece carp rod was placed in two carefully-positioned rod rests so that it pointed along the bank. The tight line ran out into the current at a right-angle to the rod tip.

At the business end of his tackle there was the feeder filled with breadcrumb cloud bait that he made himself – 'mustn't get it too wet before you fill the tube' – and attached by a link swivel to his 6-lb. line.

The trace ran on another swivel between two stops – beads from a necklace, those stops – and the hook, which looked to be a No. 12, was baited with a neatly prepared square of crumb. He told me that the bait would wave just a little above the bottom beyond the weighted feeder.

All the fish were taken on a tight line, the slightest flicker of the rod tip (painted fluorescent yellow to show up against the water) meant an instant strike. Sometimes the tip quivered; sometimes it dragged savagely round; sometimes it see-sawed and that was a bream. It was fascinating, and I picked that poor man's brains with reckless bad manners.

Humped in a raincoat against the drizzle, he would talk only as he cast. The click of the pick-up arm on his Felton Crosswind was the signal for him to stop talking. So my knowledge of swim-feeder legering, the method to end all methods, came in short sentences. Of course it was the best possible way, as each lesson was driven home with a hooked fish.

In succeeding months I hunted for feeders. As I say, they were new then, and you had to buy the whole useless float-fishing pack which few shops were stocking anyway.

I tried out the great method first on a slow river in Kent that was my concern at the time. It was a fishing match, and I soared home. Then I did it again in another match, and caught so many big bream that all they could say was they hoped I hadn't kept them all day in one net.

On another occasion we went to the Thames, which was just recovering from a dash of snow-water. My rod tip (painted yellow of course) flickered just three times. And I had three fish... good chub. No one else had anything.

Ever felt as if you've discovered a basic truth and have it all to yourself? That was the feeling I got. It was quite a shock to find it didn't last. Days came when the rod tip seemed like an immovable iron railing but even then, when everyone else was catching something, I didn't blame the feeder.

Instead of blaming it I did things that were hardly possible. I adapted it and altered it. Tried it as a slider, switched it here and there along the line, spent hours experimenting with angles of pull.

It took a lot of blank days before wisdom came and the thing found its proper place in the tackle box... to be brought out when conditions were right, and forgotten when they weren't.

Funny thing though... sometimes I have been back to that curve of the Arun in Sussex and never seen the quiet man again. I'm beginning to think he was Old Nick himself, and that he's been having a quiet tempter's laugh over my shoulder ever since.

7. The Ultimate Art
(from *Angling*, May 1968)

I must say it was a shock. Our Colonel Mac was so... well ...respectable, if you know what I mean. But I was on his side from the moment somebody spotted him grubbing a worm out of the bank of a rather exclusive, gamey, and rigidly ruled trout stream.

Since that time I've always been left quite cold by the oldest cliché in the game, the one they're always tossing up: 'dry fly purist.'

People say 'He's a purist' with despising notes to their voices – in the same way as they might say 'He's a Fascist', or 'It makes you want to vomit'.

On the other hand, there are many who wave their collapsible landing nets in your face and exclaim, with a drawl that seems to come from Olympus: 'I'm a dry-fly man you know, bit of a purist I suppose'. And as they're sighing quietly at the perfect splendour of it all, wiser though more cowardly men murmur in approval while thinking 'Here's a pompous ass' – and so pass to the river feeling great guilt because they have a bag of little red worms resting beside their box of Devon minnows.

Social equality (which means a levelling up or a levelling down, depending where you stand) is not often baulked at many points in angling. But purism, though sometimes derided as a defensive part of the class struggle, is more often applauded as art, and therefore classless.

To fish for trout with the dry fly need not be terribly expensive, of course. But usually, it is expensive, let's be frank. Yet cost is only a small part of the matter. The nub of it all is that art is associated with skill and delicacy – so if

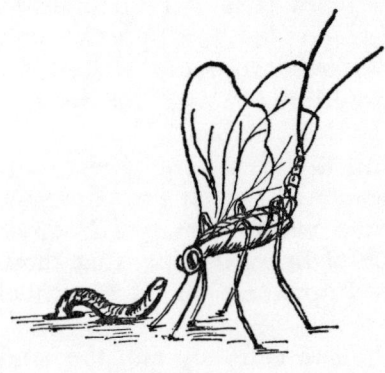

Ultimate Art

you happen to be a heavy-handed screwmaker from Walsall you'll not be happy with the dry fly, even if you can afford it. Thus the river and its pure users are saved from your elephantine cloddish presence.

This, it must be said, is an extreme view. It wasn't held by Colonel Mac looking for worms and making out he'd dropped his bottle of Mucilin. Naturally there were some who pointed out that he was only a temporary colonel ('a long time ago when everybody was that'), but the majority who noted the authentic purist achievements recorded by Mac in the fishing book, were enlightened enough to laugh and forget the incident... until future merry moments over the small glasses.

However, the point remains. Even though anybody can easily learn to fish with the dry fly. Even though the 'purist' cliché is something we are all becoming sick of... yet anybody can feel guilty. Mac felt guilty, and his friends couldn't do a thing for him.

All I know about is guilt down in the South-East, where things aren't so regal. There was once a muddy little Kentish trout stream (probably there still, though I haven't been for a long time) which survived some depressingly artificial but necessary re-stocking.

This stream was electro-fished so much that you could almost charge your car battery from the current. And the appearance of a pike was enough to cause prayers for deliverance in churches from the team of dedicated men anxious to create a new Itchen in the hopfields.

The water was divided into 'rough' or 'any bait goes' stretches, and 'fly only' stretches, a form of angling apartheid that mattered not a bit but happily fostered the Itchen myth, at least in patches.

Yet I knew, and so did everybody else, without admitting it, that if you wanted to catch the poor puny trout of this stream you used a worm. You tied it direct to a monofil trace, used a line of braided nylon that showed against the water, and moved upstream all the time, flicking the worm in front of you.

True, when the sun came up and the mud cleared a bit, a fly – any fly so long as it was wet and heavily bound with silver or gold – often worked better than the worm. Still, as any purist observer knows, the worm and this type of fly are the same... to be condemned and shuddered at.

Morning after morning, day after day, I and an equally disreputable companion took our limit of sizeable fish (shush... and more!). Sometimes it could be done casually, sitting in coarse-fishing pose, feeling the sun on the back while a farm terrier came up beside you to see what an easy dawdle it all was.

Mostly, though, this type of fishing is hard work. The long cast up, avoiding the overhanging wires that secure hop poles, taking up the slack... imagining the movement of the worm as it comes bouncing back with the current... checking it before it is sucked round submerged boulders. Then keeping the line tight as it rushes towards you... pausing just long enough as it swings round under the bank ... series of jerks in the foam... hesitation.

Now up with the rod, and he's on!

We thought it all quite a skilful business, we worm men. Didn't realise that it wasn't art though. We enjoyed ourselves, did all we set out to do, and could take on that stream any time it liked, without being defeated. Each visit meant learning just that bit more. Our knowledge of the geography of the stream bed was imprinted on our brains so that we could have drawn a chart – and put in the fish. I think I still could.

But often it happened... the grand deflation. A strange face over the bank, looking down, and a voice all hail-fellow-well-met saying: 'Are they taking?' or 'How is the sport today?'

'Oh not too bad, had three smallish ones and one near the three-quarters.'

'Have you now?' says the voice in gentle surprise. 'What fly are you using?'

'Well... a worm, actually...'

You didn't need to wonder at the sudden end to conversation. The face was withdrawn with a faint pucker of well-mannered disgust. If you'd said three smallish ones and five over the pound, the reaction would have been the same. Caught without art, those fish, and you are a guilty lout only three primeval paces away from dynamite or nets.

Digby, who often fished this stream with me, is rather sensitive in a low sort of way. So he thought of a way round these embarrassments. He called it the 'worm fly', and it wasn't the sort you buy in the shops. It was nothing more than an ordinary dry fly (with an acceptable name) tied to a large hook.

On the large hook he put a worm. He fished upstream, and if anybody came by he'd strike hard with his steely fly rod so that the worm came off. This allowed Digby to appear as a purist, fishing 'fly only'. And if, by mischance, he was unhooking a fish when somebody came by, he was adept at saying the thing had been feeding on worms and one had been regurgitated.

Watching the flyfishers making pure casts upon this Kentish stream did provide rather a fine spectacle. Only thing was, few of them caught fish. And those that were caught were never better than those we had ourselves.

It seemed to us that never a hatch of any sort appeared on the stream. A few fluttering crane flies in their season, smoke-like eruptions of gnats, the odd moth near dark perhaps – still it could be we didn't know what to look for.

But the flymen scanned the water (some even brought binoculars) and changed their flies and cast their snaky lines and went away after many blank times. Proud and brave lordlings they were, who had at least been fishing the sporting way.

A long time ago I had lunch with a very skilful gamefisher indeed. He would have got on well with Colonel Mac.

As a matter of fact, he would have offered to lend Mac his own fly dressing... except he probably wouldn't have had any with him. This man was almost as well known to top-drawer anglers as he was to the best trout. Trout were swimming in his soul, and everybody knew it. He appeared in the hotel wearing plus-fours, which proves he didn't give a fig for purism.

For years now, the more daring and the more heretical have been declaring that flies are fakes in more senses than one. They say that the science of choosing the right pattern is the merest, hopeless illusion. While Homo pauses in indecision trying to match nature as seen through his eyes, Trutta couldn't care less.

We were discussing this sort of thing over lunch, because it strikes at the heart of purism, and because my companion had knowledge that could end the cult in one terrible blast.

He loved artificial flies, this man. He revelled in the aesthetics of flies. He could classify them quicker than you can turn over the change in your pocket. But he didn't use them. Not all that much anyway. He had taken to using a bare hook.

A BARE HOOK... yes, that's what I said.

It has been demonstrated before an extremely large audience, too. And not only did he take several fish by using just a hook, but he was blindfolded as well. Fished his hook like a nymph apparently.

Those with well-stocked fly cases who like to place standing orders with secret country craftsmen, might shake with horror at this. Bare hooks! Blindfolded! Blasted circus trick, no more!

I am able to stand back from such revelations because, while enjoying my fishing with the dry fly, I shall never pin my angling life to it. Still, you must admit that a bare hook is pretty catastrophic. Where is the fascination in a bare hook? It is surely better left to airmen floating in rubber life rafts and living on mackerel, or to Eskimoes crouching over their holes in the ice.

Maybe some truths are too truthful after all. If the bare hook is the ultimate in skill and knowledge, as I am prepared to believe it is, then let's go back to the error of purism and be grateful.

8. It's In The Bin
Reflections on one man's All England
(from *Angling*, September 1968)

When they asked me to fish in the 'All England' I bought a dustbin. Nobody actually told me to go out and buy one, but after listening to all the advice from everywhere I knew that nothing else would do. It was made of red plastic and designed for litter-conscious campers, of whom there are very few. So I was able to buy it cheaply.

Those who know the 'All England' or, as it is more commonly and less romantically called these days 'The National', may understand about the dustbin. Those who don't know the 'All England' will immediately conclude that I am mad. Still, I'm not really worried, because these great angling championships, fished largely on broad, blank, canal-like waters, attract so many anglers that there can't be many people left in the country to gape at the foolishness of dustbin buyers.

When you start there are loudspeakers and as many motor coaches as there are maggots. There are tents and trailers, complimentary copies of angling journals, and pockets full of red or yellow betting slips. In 'All Englands' men dream of clearing their mortgages.

When you finish there are many cups and medals of solid gold. For the big individual winner there are rod makers and tackle men anxious to have him tell the world that without the super deluxe 'Matchsnatch' he couldn't have done it.

My understanding of these things made me buy the dustbin. The same motives inspired me to attach an obscene dangling thing to the end of my rod.

Everybody uses plenty of groundbait in the 'All England', but I think that this I used more than even the old-timers would think was humanly possible. In the days of preparation I mixed many pounds of chicken meal, bran, bread, maize meal and no fewer than three highly secret ingredients which, though useless, gave a lot of confidence. After two hours up to my elbows in mixing, the red dustbin was full.

There was only one drawback – I couldn't lift the thing.

Understanding anglers will know why I didn't take the obvious way out. The problem was an unliftable dustbin that I could just manage to stagger the length of the garden with, and the solution was not to remove some of the weight, but to go into training.

Finally I evolved a complicated double-handed snatch coupled with a puff and a snort. This got the dustbin on my shoulder. After a while I could walk a hundred yards with it in this position before I collapsed.

With this problem all but overcome I had time to consider the dangling object which for a long time now has been famous and well-used as the legering bite indicator known as a swingtip.

In the North and the Midlands, where wives never sleep with their husbands for fear of being hooked on a dream cast, the men who have these things flopping about on the ends of their rods are known as swingers. To pronounce the word correctly requires a course of instruction and involves pronouncing the 'g' as if you have a heavy cold.

But different words went out. Words to the effect that to win this particular 'All England' you needed more than just a lot of groundbait. You needed to become a swinger certainly, but it had to be the swingiest swinger that ever was, so swingy that all other mortals felt giddy at the sight of you.

Our team obeyed grudgingly because we all had mortgages and, not having any slow, brackish and breamy 'All England' type rivers to practise on, we dangled the things over a gravel pit and hoped that would do.

Many jokes have grown up about the swingtip and it's a brave man who repeats them in print, but these bits of plastic tube do work. For most people they work, anyway.

At this 'All England' the jokes were not merely about swingtips or about people who, in the name of tradition, refused to call the event 'The National'. A lot of laughter concerned a certain puffing and tottering man with a red dustbin on his shoulder. There was time for many comments as I got off the coach... because there was a mile and a half to walk to the peg.

'Whatter you going to do with that?' they shouted. They shrieked. They pointed. They made signs.

'Ahll bit ywr choofed wi'at lot lad!

'Christ, look at that chap!'...

One man rushed out of a tent and poked a movie camera at me. He almost got half a ton of chicken meal, bran etc. down his neck.

But I didn't really mind all this because on the faces of some, believe it or not, I saw looks of envy and self doubt. One chap, who had a mere ten pounds of sausage rusk in a knapsack, seemed to be watching his dreams of big money vanish with every lumbering stride I took.

That is what it's like. People will tell you other things and hold their hands on their hearts as they do so, but it's money that counts. Nobody admits it, but through the 'All England' runs a steady, lovely, avaricious undercurrent. This carries with it the one and only golden rule for all first-time 'All Englanders'. The rule is that you never, but never, ask anybody anything about fishing before the match ends. A team-mate in another coach forgot this rule and asked a silent Sheffielder what bait was best. The man came to life with a roar of incredulity. 'Faggots and mash', he said. My friend thought it might be less embarrassing to spit at an archbishop.

Advice, like good wishes, is taboo in the 'All England'. If you called out a 'Good Luck!' or a 'Tight Lines!' or some similar amateur's expression, they would turn green and vomit. There is just too much tension around. When I finally got to my distant peg just before the 'Off' and was lying on my back breathing deeply with spots dancing before my eyes, the angler pegged a few yards away on my left side looked grey with strain. He broke the rule and spoke.

'I'll be glad when it's all over', he said. I did nothing more than nod. The dustbin had done for me.

Then, from somewhere many leagues away in the flat distance, the maroons were fired and puffs of smoke hung under the wind. From all sides came the long ser-wishsh-sh and the heavy splonks as rods flashed and groundbait made the water seeth. THEY'RE OFF! In with everything! Shut out the world! It's every man for himself. Who'll get the first big bream?

'I will,' I thought, bombing the water furiously with the supply in the dustbin.

'I will,' thought the grey man on the left, as his maggots fell like rain from groundbait clouds.

The man on my right threw nothing. He was too busy striking. He went on striking nearly all day, and so did somebody else, six pegs up on the bend. And, just round the bend, something like a football crowd of spectators gathered on the bank behind a man whose face had been in the newspaper. They stayed for hours, which was depressing.

I went on bombing and casting, switching baits, probing, puzzling. Away went that mountain of groundbait. Away went hours of ghastly concentration during which nobody unscrewed a flask, lifted a sandwich or scratched his head.

Then my swingtip swung. At last! At last. Now, I thought, the match-winning, mortgage-clearing big bream are here. I struck...

There was once a great man who told everybody how he won the 'All England' with bream that finally came. People listened and were encouraged greatly. There was also another great man, some think even greater than the first, who has done an awful lot by way of telling people what to do, but he has never won an 'All England'.

During my competition this second great man fished hard and well and measured his catch in ounces, and not very many ounces at that. In fact, in deference to his greatness I will not mention them. Yet his failure gives me courage to record my own prowess.

When my swingtip swung and I struck it was to be the only bite I had that day. Oh yes, I got him. It wasn't a bream. It was a pope or, as they like to say where I come from, a daddy-ruffe. He was scarcely bigger than the legerweight. As he came out he saw the swingtip and got so frightened that he gulped the hook even further down. So rather than drag out half his innards I cut the cast and let him go.

He was released for what I like to think are humane reasons, but my conscience suggests others. At the time of course, I didn't know that the great man was going to weigh-in in ounces, and even if I had known there was still the question of the dustbin.

At least the great man hadn't gone on parade with a dustbin. He didn't have to slink away at the end of the day with a dry keepnet while trying to hide the huge, red, now empty thing behind his back.

Somehow I don't think they will ask me to fish in the 'All England' again. Maybe this indicates a second golden rule... don't advertise great things unless you can supply them.

9. Success is Relative
(from *Angling*, February 1969)

Catch me in a truthful mood and I'll admit that I have been a mediocre angler and probably always shall be. Those scenes of bold men, waist-deep in rushing mountain streams, with rods vertically above them and plunging like mad question marks while a mighty salmon makes a run that will take a whole evening to describe, fill me with admiration.
 They also fill me with cowardice. What if he falls in?
 I have been talking with a man who said he was impaled on boulders, gashed his face and was drowning for half an hour before landing that one there! As he told me, he tapped the snapshot which had him holding a darn great fish by the tail and looking remarkably dry. I guessed he'd had a hot bath and change of clothes first. But it was a big fish... 40 lb. I should say, which is what he did. This awed me a bit.
 My first salmon was taken with one foot in smelly ooze and stinging nettles and the other on a piece of corrugated iron. It was of a weight which is deserved by mediocre fishermen and took me around five minutes to land. The only thing I remember about that incident now is a sudden feeling of unstoppable power on my wrist. It felt as if the prawn had got caught up on a sunken pram being bowled along by the current.
 Yet even with a raging pram on the end I was never in danger of proving my greatness by falling in. If I had fallen in I should have let go of the rod immediately... which may be one reason why I am a mediocre fisherman. Not enough persistence. Not enough of the old single-minded purpose.

Success is Relative

But I'll talk about success with the best of them. We ordinary chaps don't have to feel small. You want to hear the club members talk about the Great Day. It was at this time of the year, just as the coarse season seemed about to peter out insignificantly, and it was unbelievable. It was also never repeated – which is why we still remember. This was the day when the river suddenly gave up what seemed to be all the fish which had ever passed along its length. All the monsters that many thought were lost, arose; all the swims that many thought were dead became treasure spots.

On the Great Day those with 'bad' pegs and resigned to working long and hard for small returns, and those with 'good' pegs expecting good returns ... all faced the miracle.

The green brollies went up. The starting whistle blew thinly over the meadows. The floats curled away. Then wonder fell upon the fishers. Catches, somebody discovered, were reaching the scales, not in pounds or tens of pounds – but pretty near hundreds of pounds.

Tragedy became triumphal, like the case of the man whose first keepnet, stuffed full, burst while he was filling his second and wondering where he could beg a third. Roach came in with fire on their bellies; the chub hit the streaming bait like brass-bound truncheons, and the dace flocked like flying fish. Every man became a giant.

The event found its way to the columns of newspapers. This made the club angry because as soon as the Great Day got into print all the anglers of Britain packed their tackle and marched to the river of golden success. And this made the anglers of Britain angry too. They found the river of gold had turned to lead again, so they went away grumbling and saying that it was all a hoax.

But, great days apart, it's a good thing for us that success must be measured in relative terms. After all, you may have more cause to pat yourself on the back after taking a six-ounce perch from an overfished pond than a pound-and-a-halfer from where the four pounders come from.

I learned this basic angling fact from newts. Mediocre or not, there can be few anglers who measure their early triumphs with newts. But I discovered a sure method. In the dun-coloured swampland known to all the boys from miles around, this muddy world which put scowls on the faces of parents and smiles on the faces of launderers, the standards were strict. Your success was judged by whether you caught a crested newt or a smoothie.

The ancient tradition was that you got down on your knees and grabbed with your hand. Nets were against the rules and rods were only for girls, whose catches didn't count. You found your quarry, you paused – aimed – and plunged. With luck there was a newt in the handful of mud.

My method was sophisticated. I used a long stick and found that by prodding their tails you could guide them in any direction until they came straight to your waiting hand and thence to the jam jar. Often I ran out of jam jars, and I'm blowed if I can see any difference between that and running out of keepnets.

But the greatest triumph I have ever seen was not with newts. It wasn't with salmon either, or with the bulging net-fulls of roach taken on the golden river. It was in a suburban park.

The scene opened when a young couple walking in front of me stopped on one of those little park bridges of Corporation rustic. There was first a quiet conversation. Then the woman took a long look at the man... and started pulling out her hair. The man looked at the woman – and began to undress.

I never really believed that I was about to see one of those sensual little acts that get into the Sunday papers via the courts. So let me say right away that she only pulled out one or two hairs and that he only took off his tie and extracted his bootlaces.

Running under the rustic bridge was a trickle of brackish water connecting two duckweed-covered ponds. In the water were sticklebacks. I heard the man claim that he would catch one within two minutes of the first cast. The woman bet he couldn't.

They told me that the stakes were high. If he did it she would let him off his promise to give her driving lessons in his car. As one who has had five years stripped from the life of a clutch by a female foot, I thought the bet fair, but dangerous.

Of course it's one thing to talk about catching something on the first cast, quite another to make any sort of cast when you've nothing to do it with. Even those who are hopelessly drugged by angling rarely stroll through the park on a Sunday afternoon with a spool of nylon in their top pockets and hooks in their lapels.

That's why he undressed. He was so keen he had a go at unravelling his socks to make a line. But modern socks don't seem to unravel quite as well as they did once. So off with his tie (what, 30 lb. b.s.?) which was attached to the bootlaces (about 10 lb. b.s.?) and for the hook length, the best strand of hair the lady could produce (10X would it be?).

With his six-foot length of line in his hand he trespassed upon the Corporation tulip bed and found a worm. Then he appointed me time-keeper, tied the worm on the hair, knelt on the rustic bridge, fixed a matchstick half way up the bootlace... and cast.

He had a fine fighting stickleback in one minute flat by my watch. No second cast and I think the fish was a British record, though I can't be sure.

That was resourcefulness if you ask me. That was real success. That was a great angler. Long may his car last.

10. Right! Let's 'Ave You . . .

With deep pride (or maybe it is just insolence) people have been known to describe themselves as 'pleasure fishermen'. By this term we usually take them to mean that not only do they refuse to enter fishing matches, but also that the competitive element kills pleasure.

At least, they infer that the competitive element brings no pleasure to sensitive, thinking blokes... the further inference being plain.

Some of them have never been able to understand this attitude. But it is a strong attitude. It makes anglers voluntarily place themselves under one waving flag marked 'Matchmen' or under another waving flag marked 'Pleasuremen'. Then they get into arguments about it.

The upshot is that uncommitted observers begin to believe that the matchman never takes an hour or two alone by the water, and that the pleasureman never feels a stir when he tells a fishless friend what he has caught.

I should have thought that most match fishers are pleasure fishers who just like to savour a little more from their catches before putting them back.

I don't know how to describe the pleasure fisher because I have always believed that every angler is that.

But not everyone thinks like this. By no means. 'Blinking pot-hunter,' says the pleasureman of the matchman... 'might just as well play bingo and be done with it!' Well, well.

I'll admit that when a steward comes along during a competition and says that so and so has got among bigger bream than you, there might be a bit of tension, if you care that much. But it is surely not the sort of tension the pleasure fisher thinks of as likely to destroy his idyllic dally with the kingfishers and rushes rustling in the wind. If anything, so and so's reported success intensifies the hunting instinct, which is a major part of the business of angling anyway.

I have often fished in competition with others, yet I have never gone around telling people how I caught one-a-minute on peg 38, or grumbling that I only had one damned eight-pound barbel in the first hour while No. 42 was getting ten pounds of two-inch bleak. Still, I suppose the nearest 'pleasureman' thinks I do.

Excessive gregariousness can be an unlovely thing, but only the worst matches are fished shoulder to shoulder. And I know many competition anglers who hardly pass two words in a day, when fishing, being lost in isolation as complete as that enjoyed by any disgraced Russian premier.

It seems to me at least that a pipe tastes just as sweet when smoked over a peg as it does when you've tramped for miles to get there first on your own special swim.

The argument that match anglers on a river mean less chance of good fish is certainly true, but this puts the spotlight on ability. Many people are surprised what those 'tiddler-snatchers' who choose to fish competitively can do when there are fish other than tiddlers for the taking. In any case, most of us have forgotten what a river without people looks like.

There is the value of solitude and there is the value of others' company. Wherever they are, all anglers should fish the day through with only the sound of the river in their ears. Radios and picnic parties aside, that is what most of them do.

Having said all this I must now add that the pleasure fishers may have some sort of point. I am not forgetting the sergeant major. It wouldn't be fair to forget him.

You have met the sergeant major? Most people have. In my case he was, I believe, once actually a corporal ... but an efficient roaring one, so the effect was the same, regardless of rank.

This was in a club to which I once belonged many years and waters ago, or so it seems. The pleasureman will tell you that matches are organised and restricted events. They were in this club. Though the stripes had long vanished from our match secretary's arm and there was only a whistle round the neck of his fishing jacket, he was good at organisation.

He was called Bill, this secretary. Or it may have been Mike or Fred, or something. Still, I am certain that once I called him 'Staff', and I remember that he took it in good part.

Our matches then always followed the same pattern. First we'd de-bus at some convenient point, leaving the coach driver either to slink away to wherever it is that coach drivers go in the daytime, or curl up on the seats with a paperback.

Then, like a guerrilla army advancing in ragged open order attack on the river, we would stumble over fields and fences to the consolidation point.

This point was always selected by the secretary, who marched at the head of us all. He was a grim veteran supported by a squelching lot of fine lads carrying buckets of groundbait, whale-size keepnets and with shoulders loaded with weapons.

At the selected spot we would, of course, begin to mill around in our wellingtons and waders – disorganised rabble that we were. Some laid their burdens down and would go off to look closely at the river, each trying to foretell his personal prospects by twin looks... one into the face of the water (which, as always, gave nothing away) and the other into the face of the sky (which, as always, gave away only what was not wanted).

Then, at last, the match secretary would slow up on his off-parade jokes, cast an on-parade eye around and march smartly to the nearest small hillock or mound high enough to raise him above ordinary men. Time to get a grip.

'Right!' he'd say. He never actually went on to call us dozy idle gents but whenever that 'Right!' came, you expected it.

'Right. Let's 'ave you then... let's 'ave you. Gather round!'

We would gather – some with behind-the-hand ribaldry, but mostly meekly.

Our matches were of the roving sort; in other words, not pegged down. So we were expected to accept the need for organisation in the interests of those who couldn't run so fast for the best swim.

'Can you hear me then?' (muttered yesses and more jokes)... 'Right.' Then he'd launch forth, official clipboard in hand and head up.

'Onemileupstream ... arfamiledown. Tenyard spacing ... and nobody leaves before 'is number is called...

'Is that clear?'

'I SAID IS THAT CLEAR? Right... each man lands 'is own fish, close allgates, no litter, onerodonehookonly – and allfishtothescales by 4.30.'

Pause. We waited.

'One more thing!' (murmurs) 'I'm not goin' to raise my voice... ANYONE WHO WEIGHS IN UNDERSIZED FISH OR GETS LATE TO THE SCALES IS DISQUALIFIED... clear?'

'Right.' He would then wave his hands in the final oration. 'Start and cease fishingonthewhistle ... and I do hope you've all got your River Board Licences.'

At last we could plunge our hands into the bag containing numbered tags (some said they could feel No. 1 by the touch) and then would wait like sprinters for an official minion to stop buttering-up the match secretary and start calling.

'One... two... three...' we moved off on our numbers. When one's own came it was like a gate opening on to sunlit meadows. Away you went under your rods to search for a swim. Already in a world of your own... providing, of course, that you didn't pass the man in front or go so far as to be unable to reach the scales by 4.30.

Fearsome regimentation it sounds, and that is probably what it was. Yet it didn't seem so bad at the time. At worse it occupied perhaps ten minutes in a long day and, as I recall them, those days were among the happiest I have ever had.

I won. I lost. I caught fish some of which I have yet to better. And on one of those days the match secretary lost his voice. Memorable occasion.

Now I belong to a different club where no military bellow ever blows under the arches of the old bridge. When I go to matches these days we have a secretary who is a man of quiet charm and does all the organisation beforehand. These matches are pegged-down and, before our arrival by car, this experienced and dedicated fellow is pacing miles of bank and having great heart-searchings about where to stick his pegs in case he should commit some unfortunate to a day in a dull swim.

But whichever club I think about, it was all pleasurable fishing. Right?

11. The Grand Return

'That looks all right for you Dad' they said, as the little lined man dragged his box on wheels up to a sedate section of bank.

Dad made a noise like 'phew', a sort of comradely noise achieved by blowing smoke past half an inch of home-rolled cigarette attached to the corner of his mouth and always only just alight.

'Don't catch 'em all Dad then!' others said, as they strode by. They went with bouncing and flowing strides past the solid home-made tackle box with two pram wheels screwed into the bottom. 'Leave some for us' and 'We know what you've got in your box, Dad!'

Dad made his blowing noise again and grinned as a man does when he welcomes such friendly ribbing as another of those little proofs that he is alive.

I watched him as he tackled-up in the sunlight, greasy cap bobbing as a chicken's comb bobs over corn. His rod was old and bent and brown, solidly laden with brass and pitted snake rings worn thin. On his blackened wooden reel was some heavy line. I could see knots in several places.

He peered through each ring as the line was threaded through. He peered more closely to attach a large plastic float with a flat red and white striped top ... and his nut-like face was only an eyelash away when he sank a large hook into a large worm.

I passed by and on down the river bank as the big red float sploshed in. Ahead were more figures casting. Long rods shining with varnish and coloured bindings sent quills

The Grand Return

skimming into the water with a swish and a wrist flick. Sunglasses were out, so were complex mechanical rod rests. The men sat in shirtsleeves rolled up from capable brawny forearms. They tensed over tins of maggots coloured red and yellow. Tiny maggots on tiny hooks... floats tapping and trotting.. deadly earnest...

It was late when I walked back that way. A day had sailed away down the river's back and the story along the bank was depressingly the same with each pace. 'Water's been dead all day'...'nothing doing'...'few small ones'. The sun had shone high and long. Lethargy had come to the river which had been about as productive as stale bath water.

Farther down the line of men weary with concentration I found three gaps... rods lying unattended and their owners nowhere.

Round the corner I found three men huddling about a tackle box on wheels. Others had also left their rods. They were running up.

At first I thought... 'the old man's gone in.' Then I saw the tip of a rod raised above the heads of the crowd... an old, brown rod, heavy with brass and snake rings. And it was bending. How it was bending!

On a lip of weed and mud jutting into the water at the base of the bank, Dad was standing in a world belonging only to him and the straining force on the end of the line.

'Easy Dad, easy!' a voice whispered. 'Keep your rod up whatever you do,' another whispered.

Dad said nothing, but blew extra hard through his minute cigarette. The fish started to run and rise and plunge. For what must have been the first time, Dad saw his float. The red and white striped tip broke water for only a second and was drawn under again. The old rod creaked round after it

'He's going to lose it!'

'Give line Dad!'

'You'll be in the weed Dad!'

The old man staggered on the ledge below the bank. The cloth cap dipped weakly. The feet slipped.

He put down one hand to save himself. Water drenched the frayed cuff of a blue and brown striped shirt. But his eyes didn't leave the rod.

At least two of the watchers rushed forward together as the wooden reel went into a spin and gave slack line. Dad stayed where he was, one foot under water, and would allow the helping hands no further than a steadying touch on the thin shoulders.

And the fish was still on. The rod was creaking again and pressure returned. Knot by knot the thick and brittle line came in as Dad slowly cranked the handles.

By now, those who had got there first were telling newcomers to 'Stand back, Dad's got a big 'un'. The fish was reeled closer. Up came the float again. Stayed up. Started to rise higher.

Under the water there was a great white flash. A wallowing sound... and the fish flapped up on the surface. It was bream, all bream. Big as a marble slab.

Dad said: 'Blimey.'

There was a hiss of indrawn breath from the onlookers.

Then Dad did a fearful thing. Maybe it was the excitement. He leaned back like a stunted tree in a wind. Right back. And with the rod handle held in both hands gave a long, long pull. His fish came in behind a bow wave.

The rod tip broke with a crack, the sort of crack that feels like a knife in the stomach.

Four landing nets rushed forwards at the ready. Four people got in each others' way. There was a confused tangle and a milling about. But Dad acted first. As the bream floundered at his feet he threw his rod down, whipped off his cap and, using it to get a grip, clutched the fish round the middle. The dorsal fin almost covered the back of his hand.

Somehow they were both hauled up to firm bank and Dad sat wet and gasping on the edge of his wheeled tackle box while the bream lay making identical gasps on the grass.

'Cor!' they said. 'Look at that then', they said. 'Stone the crows. . . .'

'Five pound' declared a young man with rolled up shirt-sleeves. Dad was wiping the slime off his cap and on to his jacket. ' 'Smore than that,' he said, puffing and wiping. 'Yeah' said the young man 'I'll bet it is.' So Dad agreed to let him put the bream in his keep net.

The net they had found in the old tackle box was almost all hole and no net. It hadn't been used for years.

I left the tight little group as they did honour. In the corner of Dad's mouth was now a long and new machine-made cigarette. In the corner of his eye the grin of a long-lost hero returned from the north.

12. Dry Line in Deutschland
(from *Angling*, January 1969)

'Your papers please', he said.. I knew what was coming.
'Fisch?' said the stocky official wonderingly, clicking a retractable ballpoint. 'Ja', I said eagerly. He smiled. Then he choked, then his ample stomach shook and he rolled about laughing. Which made things look as if they were going to be difficult.

The Bavarians are a happy people; indeed, I'd say that they were the happiest people in all Germany – particularly if you are trying to find some fishing and they can't understand you.

I tried again. 'Angle', I said hopefully. Then, with a deep breath, 'Ich bin ein Englander angler besucher.'

The man's mouth fell open and he treated my hideous, ill-remembered German in the way it deserved... with utter blank amazement that such sounds could issue from even an Englishman's lips.

'Wo ist das river?... der fluss, you know...' I said. 'So!' he said, 'Herein bitte'. I went into a large office and became the centre of a crowd of clerks all talking at the same time, and laughing and clicking ballpoints in a friendly manner.

I was about to go to the car and bring in a rod as an aid to sign language when they all seemed to arrive at a conclusion. I was doubtful when I caught the word 'schwim', and downright choked-off when they produced a map of the town's amenities and with a great flourish marked in red ballpoint a cross against the local swimming baths.

Staggering away to a waterside beer garden I downed two vast glasses of wine and slowly recovered. At my feet

Dry Line in Deutschland

the nicest, brightest, fastest little trout stream I've ever seen glittered and beckoned. Could I fish it? Could I hell! You'd think the locals had never noticed it was there.

Of course, I blame the German National Tourist Office. The Germans themselves must also take some share of the blame for not living up to the reputation of all Europeans, which is that they speak English better than we do. Before I packed my rods and went off on what was to be an angling tour I'd read the tourist office's information extremely carefully. In so-precise written English they advised you to take a rod wherever you went. Beautiful fishing, they said. Everywhere, they said. A man and his fishing rod will be deliriously happy all over smiling Deutschland, they said.

I don't know how these big and famous travelling anglers do it. They take their rods to places far stranger and far more distant than Germany and never get any trouble. It wouldn't surprise me to learn, for instance, that one of them hasn't just this moment come back from catching carp in Cathay and is just off to write a book about hooking the fighting shark of Valhalla. Of course, those who fish in exotic foreign places may well be able to speak the language, but as I sat in that waterside garden, communing sorrowfully with a waiter in terms of 'the same again', I realized that it goes deeper than that.

Well look what happened when I went to Scotland. That was last year's holiday and I took my salmon gear. They've got an awful lot of nice water in Scotland. You can't sleep at night in your tent beside the Spey because of the noise made by the salmon leaping. But there is one big drawback.

Sometimes it is the language (my English was as strange to a certain crofter in Caithness as it was to certain Germans in Rottweil), but mainly the trouble is in chasing their seasons.

I went to Scotland late to avoid the crowds and had a wild rush motoring up one side of the Highlands and down the other, finding that each river closed at a different time.

'Is it the fishing you want?' they asked as I arrived red-faced and puffing, clutching my wallet. 'We closed yesterday.' On again I motored, following information that there were still two days to go on an unknown river 150 miles north. As it took me three days to get there, owing to snow and other misadventures, I missed that too. Finally, on this Scottish scramble, I pinned down the retreating open-season somewhere in a gale near Cape Wrath and on my last day hooked four mountain boulders and had the privilege of losing four Devons.

Germany, I thought, would be different. The tourist office had assured me after all. As I sat in that beer garden I became determined that my Scottish experience wouldn't be repeated this year. I tell you that by the time I'd got half way through the Black Forest I was more determined than a cormorant who has just come off a diet. There is no temptation quite like the German rivers. Not only do you never see anybody fishing them, but they look as if nobody has ever fished them. At Berchtesgaten the water comes down from the mountains, flowing from lakes fashioned in the time of legends. It boils from the rock in flowing blue, blinding blue, sea blue with a touch of ice, and all the hotels have aquaria outside... filled with trout.

Giddy with all these sights I found that for the fishing I needed to see the Bürgermeister. The Bürgermeister had offices in the Rathaus which was covered with geraniums growing from window boxes under carved Bavarian gables. English in there was 30 per cent intelligible; my German was now 30 per cent intelligible too. We were in business.

'Ja', they said. 'Fish... so... plenty of fish.'

'Vielen Dank,' I said. Let me get at them. How much?

At this they grew stern and businesslike. My English-speaking informant pressed himself behind a desk and said: 'Your papers please.' I felt a trickle of sweat under my armpit and an escaped-prisoner-of-war feeling in my stomach. 'I don't quite verstehen you,' I said, offering my passport.

With irritation he brushed aside the golden coat of arms of Her Britannic Majesty. 'Not good,' he said firmly. I told him I had no other papers beyond ferry tickets and an old copy of *The Times*. All I wanted was a day ticket. You know, for the fishing...' angle... fisch... dieser river hier'...

'Yes, yes, that I understand,' he said wearily. 'But without the papers it is forbidden.' What blanketty mouldy old papieren was this obtuse old Herrn blathering about, I said (under my breath).

All the officials in the Rathaus immediately arose and clustered like town hall officials everywhere. I'd seen this all the way down through the Black Forest. As soon as they huddled, I went away fishless.

'Look,' I said, turning on the English charm and resolution, 'is fishing permitted here?'

'Ja, it is permitted,' they chorused. 'Good,' I said. 'Then would you kindly tell me how much I have to pay?' I began to display my small stock of marks. They pushed the money away. It was to be not fishing. Definitely no fishing.

Then somebody who looked like the patron saint of anglers disguised in Tyrolean hat with feather and leather shorts with tassels on them, murmured that he had fought against the British and would like to help me. The logic

1. One man bought the view to go with his fishing — a scene from 'Lonely Guardian'.

2. The author.

3. The red dustbin (Chapter 8).

4. Women and Fishing—in this case, the author's wife.

5. A charming contrast to the 'Monster in Weak Tea'.

6. . . . Of Charms and Fancies?

7. Not the 'Secret Stronghold', but the part of the river that can be seen from the road.

8. Winter scene — the home stream near the author's cottage.

was unsettling but the information precise. If I went to the camp site up by the lake they'd give me fishing there, he said.

I fled from the Rathaus and had a look at the lake. 'Fishing?' I asked. The man in charge said yes, 10 marks a day. This was more like it. Success at last. For the first time I felt at ease.

The lake wasn't as attractive as the river, and indeed the man who ran the camp site was doubtful about there being trout there. He told me, with pride, that they had caught a 2-lb. pike in the lake the other day and that it had impressed all the anglers. This diminished my enthusiasm slightly, but as there were only three days left of the holiday I was on my knees and begging. Permission had been found. They had day tickets after all, the crafty old Bavarians. I wasn't grumbling.

It was decided that I should come back to the campsite shop at six in the evening, pay my ten marks, and set off free and happy. Meanwhile they were so helpful that they directed me to a dung heap where all their visiting fishermen went beforehand to get worms. 'I have flies,' I said. They didn't understand and I was too pleased to explain.

So I went away and pitched my tent. Then I spent the rest of that warm afternoon happily sorting out the tackle and practising casting on the grass, to the amusement of various children. As evening came, flies were skidding up over the lake. One or two rises showed under the trees. With fishing hat, collapsible net, fishing jacket pockets filled with oil, disgorger, plastic boxes and nylon, I sauntered up to the shop carrying my rod over my shoulder.

'Guten Abend!' I called out with gaiety. 'Good evening,' they replied, recognizing the strange English fisherman. My friendly man of the afternoon got out a huge book of day tickets. It was the same sort of book as English clubs have, that English tackle shops have and that English bailiffs carry. Only the writing was different, of course, but as far as I could make out said the same things.

'Name?' he asked. I told him and he started writing. He finished writing. I paid the money. He began to tear off a ticket.

Then he paused, with the ticket half detached... 'Now your papers, please.'

I thought of sinking down in a heap right in front of him. Murderously, I asked him to explain. Slowly and simply.

He began to show me what he meant. Raising two fingers in the air like a Papal blessing he brought then down on the desk like a hammer on all my hopes.

'You have a passport,' he declared (thump)... 'to come to Germany with; you have a ticket to travel on the trains in Germany' (thump)... 'so... good... and you need also a permit to go to the fish in Germany.'

I told him in a faint voice that I'd been through all this before. Where did I get these papers? In the Rathaus? He said not in the Rathaus but at their equivalent of our rural district council offices. These were 40 kilometres away.

Right... so be it. I told him I would jump into my little English car and drive like a German all the way to the authorities. Then I'd come back tomorrow with the permit.

Snapping shut the book of day tickets he said, 'Not good.' It took longer than that to prove that I was a real angler, he said. In fact I had to supply information from England to prove that I was a real angler.

Somehow, in my simple way, I had thought that my fishing hat with flies in it was proof enough. But not at all. I had to have written confirmation from the chairman of my fishing club in England and also to produce two photographs of myself.

'This day photographs,' said the camp-site man meaningfully. Not old ones. He said that after filling out a form in the presence of the authorities they would then stick one photograph upon it and file away the other. Then I would wait 48 hours, or maybe 72 hours for the documents to be processed.

'After this', he said (snapping shut the book of day tickets), 'you may fish any place in Germany.'

He could see that my stiff upper lip was faltering and laid a kindly hand on my arm. 'In Germany,' he told me, with a touch of humour, 'we need papers for everything. Isn't it the same in England?'

'No it isn't,' I said sternly. I was about to expand on the

freedom of England when I checked myself, and thought about it. What if some happy angling Bavarian suddenly got out of his Volkswagen on spec at Stockbridge? How would he get on, I wonder?

The idea consoled me all the way back down hundreds of miles of autobahn.

13. In Time of Flood

The river has been lost in past days. It seems we have not been without rain for weeks, months... aeons. Now disappointment and impatience hang as heavy as the clouds. Instead of the clean, winter-coloured stream running true through the meadows and down the salmon ladders it has evolved into a lake, or rather a series of lakes. Somewhere in the middle of this new circlet of water sprawling over grass and dyke is the true river, its full force still rushing. But you can't see it.

Even the sidestreams, usually low and red with iron, are filled and bursting and our anglers are chafing. George has cancelled the club competitions and moans that 'it won't be down for a month'.

The wide arches of the stone bridge have been reduced to small semi-circles perched on foam and debris, while the sound of deep, disturbed water in a hurry overlays even the tyre swish on the road.

Three times I have been to this new lakeland with packed basket, hot flask and some worms that have been so long scouring themselves that they are as bright and hard and tantalising as diamonds. And three times I have come away without unpacking a rod. Meanwhile, the peak of grayling time is passing.

George reckons there are one or two spots where a good floodtime fisher might angle with hope, but these are obvious spots and every searcher cannot fail to miss them. So if you were not up early then you may as well go home.

Amid so much pessimism the optimists stand out. Cobby Cottar who walks around with a book of day tickets and

In Time of Flood

'looks after' a weir pool and a mile of bank is finding his qualities stretched to the limit, but the fact doesn't show.

For most of the year Cobby does an amazing public relations job on his water. He looks like Mr Pickwick, everyone's idea of Mr Pickwick – dumpy and red and bouncing with enthusiasm. After meeting Cobby and fishing on his stretch you cannot fail to have a good day. He tells you that.

'You'll get some good ones there,' he says. Or 'What's that? Not caught anything yet. I don't believe it. But never fear they'll come on this afternoon.'

But now Cobby is hard put to keep up with his tradition of zest and confidence. Anglers down from distant cities are splashing dangerously through water while not knowing they are yards away from casting distance of the actual river.

They roam the brimming grassland like coolies in a paddy field and the wind comes in on a spray of rain, turning their faces blue and making them huddle down into cold collars.

In fact there is a spot on Cobby's water, a spot that, at floodtime, can open up the golden horn of grayling and dace. This information has been whispered to me in confidence by the kindly local newsagent. He drew me a map all over the white part of a Sunday newspaper advertisement.

Cobby knows the spot too. I caught him telling it to a stranger who has come down from some far subtopia for a week's winter fishing. Cobby took his arm, sold him a ticket, and set him carefully in the spot. I was only minutes behind, but that's long enough to miss out.

This spot for a floodfisher's carnival on our river is, in normal times, a wide, easily-fordable run of shallows below the weir pool.

The water now though is roaring out from the hatches. No longer chalky white. Muddy brown. Swirling away in a racing arc, its force is spent largely in a deep channel on the far bank, while the rest flows more steadily over the shallows.

Depth here, in quieter times, is about a foot. At this time it is three feet. 'Just right', said the newsagent. 'Ideal and perfect, you'll get a good day', says Cobby, raising his voice above the lashing of his wonderful water and tearing off a soggy ticket.

The young man from far away doesn't fish as he should though. For some reason he is fishing this rare spot with a float leger. Poor man. Unable to break with his experience on slow breamy rivers he is throwing away his great opportunity. Our river is never slow and now it is an angry dragon.

Cobby's brief never takes him as far as advice on tackle; perhaps that is why he has so many friends and his encouraging smile is so welcome. But the newsagent, who knows the right way, and George, who has seen it too, both believe that this privileged stranger would be just as well off fishing with a tennis racquet. He is not going to catch anything and, behind him, the queue of those who could must stay restive.

The right way to fish these newly-deep shallows is with worm and small float. But the float must be held back so that the bait comes first to the grayling, the line tight from bait to float, float to rod tip. And all is done by feel rather than sight.

Yet... there it goes... mighty cork float and a ton of leger... plop into the rapids. Oh, the crime of it!

Back on the bridge another angler is fishing an eddy caused by the bankside arch-pillar breaking the back of the flow. It is a small whirlpool boiling under savage upthrusts of current. From the bridge you can see a short way below the surface and it is like the crater of some watery volcano. Leaves and twigs, even whole branches, come bubbling up. They appear in the murk, turn, and are sucked away.

The angler's float is spinning and skidding and his bait is following. Only a starving fish which has managed to come to terms with St Vitus' dance could possibly catch the jigging maggots.

Now... if he were legering, he might stand a chance. My rods are in the car. I'm leaving them there.

A Dormobile packed with young faces draws up beside me on the bridge. During the past hour I have seen it parked uncertainly, forlornly, in several places. The windows are steamed up and the occupants are too depressed to get out. There comes a loud shout – but heard only as a small squeak above the sound of water.

Cobby's stocky figure can be seen hurrying down to the shallows, a blob of black oilskin scampering against a grey glacier.

The driver jumps out of his van. He is behind me as I hurry from the bridge. Cobby and his float-legering protegé are tense and triumphant. The angler's rod is up and bent; the leger is bouncing up against the float and down to the stop shot as the fish runs from the centre of the shallows to the bank. Cobby's face is a grin. Satisfaction crackles from him.

Then the bent rod straightens and the angler swears, stricken to his soul. But Cobby says 'Ah you've lost him ... get in again. There's plenty more where he came from.'

'Probably a big barbel' says the driver of the Dormobile wisely. He runs back to the bridge where the vehicle's engine is still ticking and five faces are still peering through the steamed up windows. The clutch is let in harshly and they all disappear at speed. Maybe they will find big barbel where they are going. They expect to.

For a second I feel I should get my rods from the car. Cobby is making an oration: 'You've got to know my beautiful river ... it isn't the muddy Thames. It's beautiful and clean. But I'll say you've got to know it'.

Through the clouds there's a faint hint of brightness. Enough to put a sparkle on the sunken meadows. It *is* a beautiful river. Everything is forgiven.

14. Once, They Never Were ...

I can't quite remember when it happened, though it was probably during that time in adulthood when I ceased to be a boy and almost became a cynic. But happen it did. The collapse of a legend, bringing with it the bitter ending of artificial hope. In short, I discovered that fishing-tackle dealers are shopkeepers.

Or, to be more accurate, I should say that tackle-dealers are shopkeepers first and anglers second in the best cases, or anglers not at all in the worst cases.

At one time I put them firmly in place among all the people I most wanted to know. In those days my ambition had soared way beyond the red-throated sticklebacks living in the park duckpond and was concerned with gudgeon living below a Kentish weir.

That weir once seemed a gigantic, thunderous place, yet it soon became like any other weir. All too soon. And when the great pounding sheaves of water tossed into the pool finally appeared as not really very dangerous or very thunderous, I still clung to my belief that all the charm and knowledge of angling lay with the man behind the counter.

The window of the tackle-shop shone out between a greengrocer's and a tobacconist's crammed together on the brow of a hill. It was always on my route, and it always offered three separate delights.

The first delight was the window itself. What artistry there was in the display. Long looks at the packets, the rods, the bottles of dark varnish, the whole spread of angling paraphernalia. Then back for longer looks.

Second delight: the moment of entering the shop. Hand

on the doorknob, slight shake because the door always stuck a little, the trinketty clack of a dulled and worn-out bell... and in to the smell of rods and netting and more than the eye could ever encompass in a single visit.

The third delight was, of course, the greatest. Speaking to the tackle-dealer. Actually talking to him of No. 12 crystals to 6X. Bliss!

Behind the counter was the man with the limp and a fishing club badge. I was sure he treated pennies with reverence, and gave me man-to-man debate over this float or that. If I saved, and brought silver, I could earn a long piece of decision-making and, yes, he'd take my silver and make sure no-one else bought the only rod in all the world ... and I could come back after my birthday with the rest.

Now, looking back, I am sure it couldn't have been like that. Knowing what I know now it couldn't have been. Could it? I wish I were wrong. Anyhow, I went back to that shop a few years ago and found it had become a place which sells washing machines, T.V. sets and irons. There's a new plastic shopfront where once was blistered wood, and the door is all glass and doesn't stick.

Forgetting nostalgia and boyhood paths, I refuse to fall into the error of believing that tackle dealers have changed. I know that things are never what they were, so logic demands that my tackle dealer with the limp be placed alongside those who serve me now. The picture isn't half so pretty as the one that faced the captivated boy.

Take The Case of the Innocent Angler as an example of legend destroyed. I could compile a dossier of such cases but this one will do because it is fresh in mind, having happened only a short while ago.

The Innocent is an aggressively countrified townsman who wears tweed hats which always seem hard and new. He talks loudly about not knowing much about 'this fishing game', and the uncharitable, or the short-sighted, might despise him. But his heart is in the right place and he needs guidance.

But he doesn't get guidance. The tackle dealer in the large town nearest my own small town holds out a false helping hand. It is horrifying to watch.

'Rods', says the Innocent, all determined.

'Rods!' says the dealer, happily leaving my attempt to remember if I need 25 yards of monofil.

'What sort did you have in mind, Sir?'

'A good strong one', says the man, 'for the one that gets away', and grins a ghastly grin as if he had out-Oscarred Wilde.

The dealer puts out the only feeler that matters – 'What sort of price did you want to pay?' Straight down to it like that. He knows his man.

'Oh I don't know ... what do they come at these days?' says the Innocent. He spins the display turntable so that all the price tags fly gaily about and the nodding tip of a beach-caster almost knocks off his new hat.

The gleam grows behind the dealer's spectacles. His small conscience finally gets him to ask the man what type of fishing he had in mind. The customer, who likes the look of a glass boat rod, but thinks the thirteen foot match rod has got nice binding, asks whether or not there are any salmon about.

To give the dealer full credit he does try his fatherly chat (stage 1) for obvious beginners (upper middle-income bracket), but he doesn't try too hard. The man isn't the easiest fellow to get on with it's true. He blusters gratefully about how his tweed-hatted grandfather once stunned 'em all for one glorious season on an unknown river in *Sweden* ... then he buys a tubular steel giant, the most expensive rod on the stand.

'Just wrap it up', he says. 'Don't know much about this game. You say it's a good rod and that's alright by me. Rely on you. Hope the wife approves' (and winks and laughs).

Not the easiest man to get on with, as I say. But this is plain, unvarnished robbery. And it has gone on. He has been in many times, buying, and buying, and buying.

To my knowledge his purchases have included a fixed-spool reel of enormous complexity; a fixed-spool reel of less complexity but greater expense; a set of weatherproof garments of the sort you find advertised in only the best field sports magazines (the dealer put in a special order for those) and a shooting-stick (it was beside the pictures of weatherproofs in the catalogue).

A landing net – about right for minnows; a keepnet – obviously for the same purpose; a tackle box of inscrutable Oriental origin and designed, one imagines for Oriental builders' tools rather than tackle: a host of bright flies – the dealer said coarse fish sometimes take them; a heavily striped aluminium-framed folding deckchair and one of those 'Junior Fisherman' sets done up in cellophane and with a box more useful than the contents... the dealer said it was 'just the thing to get Malcolm interested'. Malcolm, he had discovered, was the Innocent's son.

I have also seen the sale of two rod-rests bristling with screws, a bundle of bite-detectors looking capable of easy transformation into electro-fishing outfits, and just about every new device for depositing groundbait, pressing breadcubes, clearing weed and frightening fish which the dealer could rush into his window.

The dealer is not the sort to lose any sleep over this. Even if he saw what I have seen his nights would pass peacefully. Yet I have seen the Innocent Abroad.

He sat on the bank, with Malcolm sporting spottily in a bright blue tent at his elbow. The aluminium deckchair was perched over a rather nice roach swim. His expensive rod, armed with at least 12 lb. b.s. nylon was sticking straight upwards and waving in the breeze. A bright marker buoy of a float bobbed on the water and suspended a good four inches below it was a size four carp hook to twisted nylon braid. The bait was a plastic sand eel.

I passed with a nod of deceitful comradeship and noticed his latest angling buy. A Radio 1 babble roared upwards from the transistor radio and covered the fields in noise.

It may be unfair to blame the tackle dealer for this terrible state of affairs. He must take some share of the responsibility though. If he hadn't got the silly fellow so blinded by gadgets at the start of an angling career, then the novice might have caught fish. He might have progressed. He may still progress, though I don't think he will. The radio is a substitute for the taste that died without ever being cultivated.

You may say that this tackle dealer was not representative of his kind. Thinking of my lame man stumping in rosy retrospect, I'd like to agree. But a myth is a myth and dies hard, although I admit that some dealers seem slightly aware of what never was. But only slightly.

Some dealers do look as if they spring from the reminiscence of people who seem to have been fortunate. Old gnarled countrymen who tie their own flies to secret and deadly patterns and have names like 'Snatcher Sam' or 'Old Codge who does a bit of poaching on the side', and always know where the fish are lying.

This is all merely an echo of a legend. We like to think that there are characters who know all the wrinkles, men you are advised to contact, men who have never heard of the profit motive but live for the blessed art and good angling conversation and 'Quietly sir, I've something for you under the counter'.

It is, I fancy, a cruel lie. I know them and I've found them out. They start off as men who are making a living from what they love, but it doesn't ring true. After a while their talk grows shorter and is likely to lead on to the nasty Japanese tackle makers, thrusting trade in your face and not seeming like angling at all.

I know of one who impresses new or casual customers by calling regulars by their Christian names and saying had they heard about Charley's big day 'on the deeps' or Fred's big win up north somewhere?

This type of dealer is a real, genuine, paid-up member of the local club. He keeps abreast of the local fishing talk and will even draw you a picture on the back of a hook packet, of the latest reel he has ordered. At first glance you think you've found the man you'll buy from for ever so long down the angling years. A man who lives for the sport. Fellow you can yarn with, fill a pipe with, and depart from empty-handed.

It is unsatisfactory to find that you never actually see him fishing, and worse to learn that no-one has ever actually seen him fishing. Though it may be rumoured that he packed some rods when last he took the family for a seaside holiday.

And it is sad but true that if you do fill a pipe and look like departing empty-handed, then you'll find his fishing talk getting slower and in his eye appears a look that turns out to be barely concealed impatience.

Still, search on if you must. Stick at it. In desperation you are likely to go completely round the bend, and expect to find the genuine stuff all legendary tackle dealers are made of in your large and escalatored department store.

In a section divided from the garden shears and car seat covers by the odd tackle-maker's advertisement (usually a swinging, leering cardboard fish or something) you find a display cabinet so ill-stocked that you wonder why they bother. Immediately you can sense that you're not going to find whatever it is that you want. Nothing anyone could possibly want survives in the pathetic collection of odd rods, polythene bait containers, bakelite reels and spools of nylon by makers you have been warned about.

However, at least the tackle dealer here is something different. He could be young and just moved 'Carpets'. He probably has the store's badge in his lapel (instead of a club one) and he's certainly very quick at reading what it says on labels so that he can tell you what the things are meant to do.

Of course, if you can stand horror greater than this, then the tackle seller in such places is quite likely to be not the young man from 'Carpets', or even a young man at all.

It could be, and often is, a Woman.

But this thought I can't consider for long. Though she says, all sweet and eager to help, that 'the traveller said these were very good', all true fishermen must pass politely, but shudderingly, from her sight.

No, gentle brothers, the lame man walks no more and pennies are not wanted. Follow me, and become severely practical about things. I am at last content to salvage what I can from the sweet illusion now lost. I patronise the dealer who is always the last to run out of maggots, or who serves the anglers first, before those who want an electric racing car, a game of ludo or a camera.

15. Women and Fishing
(from *Angling*, September 1970)

So why was I casting into this goldfish pond? I'll tell you: I've recently been getting interested in women again. And in case anybody thinks of something funny to say... it's been said already. My interest has been entirely scientific and inspired by the fact that none of my best fishing friends is a woman.

In fact, when I last looked, none of my casual fishing friends was a woman either. And they didn't know any women. So where has the species gone?

I began looking for women anglers in such likely places as country garden parties, held in aid of worthy fieldsports causes. At one there was a stack of old brook rods brought down from an attic in the sort of house occupied by people who can afford to leave umpteen-pounds-worth of delectable cane in attics.

I paid something interesting in notes, took a rod and cast for a long time at rubber rings floating in this goldfish pond. The idea was to win a handmade cane toast rack. After missing the rings so often that I had to make a joke about really trying for the goldfish, I sidled close to the lady who beat me. Looking into her eyes (iron blue) I let out my most charming smile.

Then I went away, believing that she would have been much happier breeding bassett hounds or opening village fêtes.

In a less expensive manner I went on to study club match results, because everybody kept telling me that more women were coming into angling. There's always a 'ladies' shield' after all, and the last one I saw presented was won

Women and Fishing

by a lady who could tread on my cloak any time there's a puddle. She got 2 lb. 6 oz. 4 drm., I remember. The trouble was that she'd gone to a whist drive and her husband came up to accept the trophy for her. His last match weight had been 4 oz. 4 drm.

Roar of jokes and a wooden spoon... 'Aye, Aye, Harry, who wears the trousers in your house then?'

Being scientifically inclined, I sighed a tragic sigh. I've heard the stories, you see; the tales we like to tell on a hundred riverbanks and all proving that the 'little woman' really does wear the trousers.

Digby was an angler I once knew. Afflicted by the courtship disease, he walked the riverbank hand in hand with his girl and saw nothing but the fairest face in all the world. The bream were bubbling so hard that you imagined them swelling up, but he didn't notice.

Later, as the grip slackened slightly, he told me with real innocence that he'd found the girl in a million. She was deeply interested in fishing, he said. She wanted to 'take it up'.

What could I do but agree? Of course he was a lucky chap. And I think she meant it at the time. Certainly Digby saw the years ahead as a period of perpetual kingfisher blue. Together they would roam the meadows discussing dough bobbins or the invisible merit of white floating lines; together they would fish their lives through, interpreting tench bubble messages. And over the cocoa on winter nights they would talk of dead herrings, or snap tackle, and how long to delay over the strike.

She came to the river dressed in the latest angling fashion. Neither concentrated very well; she was busy weaving birds' nests in monofil, he busy untangling them. He enjoyed the symbolism, she made it reality. After the wedding he did not appear by the river at all.

I went rushing away to the dark eddies where misogynists lie and developed complex reasons why angling and women don't go together. And then I developed a complex theory for when they do go together. It was a theory concerning genetics and the absence of lipstick...

Now I find it an unwise theory, probably unsound and certainly dangerous. Anyhow, the true anglers I have seen among women caused me to change my mind.

There have been just three of them – all I could find in a long and careful search. The first was the wife of a chemist, a kind sensible woman who could have been anybody's mother. She badgered her husband for special concoctions to add to her groundbait.

The second was a widow who looked like everybody's charming grandmother – and I actually saw her rub a ferrule in her neatly done hair. Case proved. Until then I'd considered this hoary handy hint an obvious mark of man's superiority.

The third woman angler had children so well trained that they would stay with father a mile away rather than approach her when the dace were going well over a long trot.

There was, at one time, a fourth on my list. And I maintain, against all evidence, that she would have made it – except for a most terrible traumatic experience.

My wife had reached the stage when she could put a maggot on the hook, but wouldn't do it with a worm. Most anglers will understand that this was a mighty big step forward just the same. Anyhow, at this particular time she was float fishing. Down the swim it went, tottered, hovered, paused... and then dived away. My wife struck firmly.

'I've caught something, I have really'.

The rod was bent and she started winding. It was at this point that I thought it all looked a bit odd. Things didn't seem quite right: the rod was bent, certainly, but the weight equally certainly on the end was not doing anything – like trying to get away.

I had a strange feeling. She didn't. With a heave she stepped back. Then heaved again, stepped back farther to see what she had caught...

It came out of the water like a fiend from the grave, dripping with horror. An eyeless skeleton with jaws agape and tatters of moulding flesh clinging to a shape that was only faintly fishlike. The hook was caught in the upper jaw, where the lip should have been, as if the dead had made a last jaded snap and the next one would be at her arm. Once it had been a perch, before it became a ghoul and sank to the bottom to rot. Now it was the kind of creature children have in mind when they think that something has crawled into bed with them.

My wife screamed a scream that rose with a slap against the clouds. The flexibility of rods and the law that says every action has an opposite reaction, being what it is, the thing immediately soared towards her. She saw it coming, jaws agape. She dropped the rod and ran away to the horizon, where she stayed, shouting that I was going to chase her with it.

That was the last time she went fishing. No, of course it wasn't my fault. The thing worried me, too, though I looked quite calm as I kicked it back into the river and moved quickly to another swim.

I am certainly not going to suggest that the reason women and angling don't go together is... men.

16. The Fact About Digby

There may be recorded somewhere the fact that an angler has tripped on a banana skin and been taken through a jerky slapstick comedy routine ending in others' laughter and his disaster... but I doubt it.

Bananas, of course, are useful things for taking along with the sandwiches and I even know people who say they catch chub on them. However, as river banks generally exist in a certain sogginess and to work properly a banana skin needs to lie on a hard surface or, at least, not to be trodden on with cleated soles, they are not a major hazard.

There are plenty of things lurking by the river for our discomfort, and the only point about mentioning banana skins is that the effect of these other natural hazards upon the human form is often similar. Digby, I am glad to say, knows far more about this than I do.

Digby is a man who was once a boy with me. He weaned me from caterpillars and stone-axe making by putting my mind on crucian carp. He has always looked the least accident-prone of individuals.

Nowadays he shares his life with a beard of remarkable exactness and cultivation. There is also a deerstalker hat that looks, upon him, almost the result of evolution.

Such a fellow as Digby – lean, sensitive and with the beard brushing him against intellectualism – is naturally inclined towards a quite unreasonable neatness. Nothing, you think, could make him look accident-prone. So perhaps it is just that he is unlucky. Despite his qualities and bearing it is a sad fact that he is more vulnerable than others to all the things that act as anglers' banana skins.

I am not talking about the small things, you understand. Not such things as brambles and nettles. When we go fishing he always walks ahead holding an elegantly packed tackle box with trim carrying handles and, whatever the wilderness, the biggest brambles and the strongest nettles always seem to float humbly aside and lay down their spikes at his approach.

Being somewhat stouter and always more heavily laden, I flounder along behind – and awake the blasted things from the slumber he has put upon them. Every time they rise up with sudden energy and grip me. I think they do it in cheated rage. By the time we get to open country I am hot, sweating, puffing and torn. At such times I admit to private distress at the superbly unaltered set of his deerstalker.

Even after a hard day's fishing from inaccessible spots in all weathers (though neat, he simply dotes on inaccessible spots in all weathers) he always manages to climb into train or car without a speck of mud on him, and looking ready for cocktails at seven.

This I could never understand. It baffled me for a long time. Then I discovered that Fate was reserving him for bigger things . . banana skin things. For me and a thousand others it is brambles and nettles, or perhaps the occasional collapse of a seat basket; for him the world of hazard is laid out like a red carpet which, being stepped on, rolls you up inside.

If you regard an angling tragedy as something that stops you fishing, or limits your chances, then Digby gets tragedy right in the neck. There's the time that he needed a keep net desperately for a big bream. He borrowed one which was brand new and smelling of oil and complete with meat skewer for holding it to the bank. But the bank was soft and within five minutes the Billy Bunter bream had the skewer out and was pushing off downstream with the net still round him. That episode cost Digby a badly negotiated £3.50.

Then there's the time we were both heading for a certain spot. We knew the mood of the river, and the swim was and is a favourite one. We also knew that it was the only one. So we were racing. And let no-one who fishes in company say that he has never done the same.

One swim. Two people. Even start. It was civilised business of course. I waited until he had got his rods out of the boot, and he waited while I put my wellingtons on. All the same, it was still two minds with a single thought.

Side by side we walked at gradually increasing speed. The closer to the river, the more we talked of other things while that one deep run, that hook packet crushed among that certain root-hollow for years, were all waiting for the first to arrive.

One fence to go. Ten yards beyond was the swim. Untenanted. Good. Breath coming in gasps... 'got any worms?'... hot sock getting crushed round my instep... I put my basket down. Home! Now to make it look as if the tape hadn't yet parted.

Then, behind me, I heard a sort of squeal. I turned. There was Digby in tragedy. Hanging upside down on the wire fence, he was.

It was one of those tallish fences made from four or five widely set strands of smooth wire, secured through notches in metal posts. It was not a hazard at all disposed to lie down at the approach of a Digby.

'By George!' he said. Just like that. 'By George!'

How he did it I don't know. His hands and feet were on one side, his body curled over the top and his head hanging through the wire at the other side. His rods were everywhere and the toolbox was jammed between his arm and his back. But most peculiar thing of all... his deerstalker was still on his head. Gravity-defying that hat. And at the correct angle too, inches from a group of venomous cow pats.

Later he loped off past the coveted swim, looking as though it couldn't have happened, and fell to his thighs in a drain ditch forded by a single rotten plank.

His grandest effort, though, was much more spectacular. For dignity's sake he doesn't talk about it except to me, and he only does that because we both share a cringing fear of anything larger than a lamb... and this was a rather large bull.

It happened in Norfolk. And Norfolk, as Digby had cause

to remember, is a wide sort of place, and treeless. Ahead was a vast meadow with one gate. He went through the gate first.

The reason I didn't go through the gate was that a rod rest had slipped through a hole in the old pensioned-off bag I keep just for rests and landing net handles. So I went back to look for it while he went on. Into the field. Far into the field.

A faint sound which I'll swear was a windborne 'By George!' came to me as I got back to the gate. Far away in the middle of the pampas-like spread of grass was a small speck. A still speck. Unmoving. Off to the right of it was a larger speck. A much larger speck. And it was moving ... fast, with a sort of rumbling noise.

Even at a distance it looked absolutely certain that the two specks would meet with a nasty crunch. But Digby, putting his angular shanks to work, drew away and flew towards the only tree in all that expanse of field and marsh. He ran for it as though it were the only tree left in the world. That's what it looked like. And, of course, it was.

Stunted and small and leaning over the river, the tree waited as the ground moved under the bull's hooves. Digby flapped into it like a garish giant stork and fluttered in a teaming mass of beard and Harris tweed upwards to the thinnest branches.

I crossed the river and moved up the safe bank to condole with the face among the leaves. Between us was a decent width of water some eight feet deep.

Digby said By George and what the hell was he going to do now?

The bull said a grumble and looked up.

After ten minutes Digby said he thought he was slipping and I was discarding extravagant ideas like running for a farmer some thousands of miles or more away, or doing something really tricky like stunning the bull with a carefully cast coffin-lead.

Fifteen minutes later Digby did slip. He slipped down to about three feet from an angry red eye. The deerstalker planed down to the mud at the animal's feet and was trodden on.

All this excited the bull quite a bit, but after taking it out on the deerstalker and pushing it almost out of sight in the mud, he seemed to get bored. Finally he decided that the chances of finding another deerstalker were better over the other side of the field.

Digby's long retreat from the tree was made with great daring and cunning along the line of the river bank. He moved like a commando, half in and half out of the water so that a bull's eye view from the distance would have been a bobbing black beard appearing in sudden rushes to collect scattered contents of tool box, rods, thermos flask, before the final scamper to the gate and safety.

We never recovered the deerstalker. However, Digby had a new one some weeks later when we rushed for the first and last long-distance train non-stop to a new river, caught it, sank back in the seats... and found he had left his rods at home.

17. What Is It . . . A Sprat?

There is no point in being fed up about Smith. He is, you might say, a fact of life. But beware of him all the same. There are people who walk by rivers and people who fish in rivers . . . and between the two the gulf is wide and dangerous to cross. I reckon it is worth remembering this when your non-angling friends announce that they can't understand what you see in the 'game'. Mind you, my Smith wasn't that sort.

But we must be even more cautious and alert when our non-angling friends say they are thinking of 'Having a go' themselves. My Smith was that sort. And I suffered. How I suffered. So take warning.

Those who merely walk by rivers no doubt see beauty and poetry, find relaxation, even inspiration. Anglers see these things too, or many of them do. Yet there is more isn't there? Much more.

We are divorced from ordinary water lovers. Though it seems a small thing now to feel that tug inside at the sight of waving weed while looking deep into a chalk flow it is, in fact, a rare thing indeed. That sudden shadow over gravel, or that lazy spattering of bream bubbles; the knowledge of how the current moves food from this place to that, these feelings come from an angler's awareness. But don't breathe a word about it because all this isn't easily acquired.

The late (now long late) and great (still great) Captain L. A. Parker, expert practical angler, once advised that your reply to the man who comes up to you on the bank and says he can't see anything in that 'game' should be . . .

'I'm glad, there are too many anglers already'. Ah, a sad truth.

All the same, that may be a good snappy thing to say, but what do you tell the man who comes up and declares that he's going to give the 'game' a try? I'll bet my new and beautiful salmon spinning rod against anyone's battered converted tank aerial, that the average angler's reaction to the approach of a new recruit is one of extreme pleasure.

Well, it is satisfying isn't it? Be honest. Here's old Bloggs from the golf club, of Brown who sits next to you in the office – or, in my case, here is Smith whose lawn mower you borrow and who gives you his garden worms. Here they are, more or less asking you to let them in on one of life's pleasures. Who could resist such a chance? For a moment at least you are a small king with a big bounty to bestow.

So you make careful plans, thinking that it is rather like beginning your own angling career all over again. One or two books cannily selected and loaned... one or two trips to places where the fishing is not demanding... then take him to the tackle shop so that the gear he borrowed from you can be replaced by his own. That, you think, is how it will go.

You think!

If it hasn't happened to you yet, beware, as I said. Because it rarely goes like that. You could almost say it never goes like that.

Notice here that I'm not thinking about teaching your son to fish, or teaching Bloggs', Brown's or even Smith's son to fish. That is a different matter entirely. That can be genuinely satisfying (and the whole business is thoroughly selfish, of course), for with the young and keen you have a fair chance of succeeding.

With those out of their teens you have a lesser chance. There are exceptions I know, but in the later years the prospects of finding converts who think about fishing as you do are about as hopeful as beating Richard Walker's carp record after breaking the ice on the local paddling pool.

You might just catch a fifty pounder with the snow

falling – by foul-hooking him while he's dormant and in a trance. And you might, just might, hook your enquiring would-be angler by similar foul means.

Alright, let's take our Smith-type fishing. Isn't it obvious right away that you are going to need to be underhand? Of course, I don't mean that you dive into a hidden keep net when he's asleep in the sun and artfully fix a two pound chub to his hook, then wake him up shouting 'You've got a bite!' That is too crude, and anyway it is an outrage against conscience.

No, 'foul' has a subtle definition in the case of Smith. It means cutting corners; it means giving him INSTANT SUCCESS because if you don't you can see he's going to throw the rod away and go rushing back to his lawn mower.

I admit that this is all very unpleasant and downright unsatisfactory, as we all know that INSTANT SUCCESS isn't a good thing. You know, also, that whatever success you give him he can see something larger or more exotic on any fishmonger's slab. And the joy of catching fish doesn't last if it comes too easily.

After all, remember when we started all those years ago? Remember the long blank days? We chafe at similar events now but in those early times even blank days were delicious. There was the period when we used laughably strange tackle in ponds and canals that we later learned needed to be fished at five feet instead of five inches. Recall, in the name of tolerance, the tense anticipation that preceded each of those blank days – the feeling that the night would never pass, that you'd miss the train, or that it would rain.

And what about the time you bought a 6X cast by mistake instead of tying straight on to the 12 lb. b.s. braided binder twine... and so caught your first monster roach which was all of a solid and breathtaking four ounces? All this was a long apprenticeship, a happy learning that angling has little of patience in it and many heart-pounding hours of hope.

Now here's your Smith. Here he is, waving a cheerful goodbye to his pitying wife, striding along with you to the car and shouting back over his shoulder that he'll be returning with a whale ... ha ... ha. Here's your Smith propping open the car door with the rod you lent him (old, but you still love it) while upsetting a tin of maggots and, with a grimace, asking you to pick the nasty things up.

How do you tell him, as he stands at the edge of a lovely, easily-fished river, that here is a favourite swim where the bream move to groundbait within half an hour and that, even now, the big greedy fellows are prospecting the bottom?

'I can't see anything,' he says, looking down into the water. 'They must have heard I was coming'. They probably did, but you laugh too because normally he's a nice intelligent bloke – over the lawn mower.

Let's face it, we don't expect Smith to creep up on his belly in the fashion some of our more esoteric textbooks recommend. We don't even expect him to sit entranced at the joy of unravelling gremlin-packed yards of tangled nylon from his reel. We are fair-minded, tolerant angling men and, to be just, most of us still curse in an evil way at birds' nests. But somehow, stupidly, we don't expect him to regard it all as a huge joke or to be so... well... astonishingly irreverent.

Of course, your Smith might be the serious sort. There are serious new-angler Smiths. Serious or not though, the time will come – as soon, perhaps, as an hour after getting him settled by the river – when he needs to catch fish.

'Nothing's happening', he says. He says it with some surprise.

You look up from your own swim. It is an inferior swim yours, but selected with magnificent altruism because it was close enough for you to keep an eye on him. So you look up, and get up, and hover over his shoulder.

Smith is obviously losing interest, and losing it fast. You shouldn't have tackled up for him, though of course you had to. Neither should you really cast for him, though of course you are going to because it is more than you can stand to see him grimly eyeing his float as it gyrates at his feet with the hook, bearing a roach-sucked gentle, sticking into the float cap.

So you take his rod and cast. 'Thanks. Can't get the hang of it', he says. You cast again. And again. Because the sun's

What Is It ... A Sprat? 91

gone in and the rain's coming and you know that rain is going to be fatal.

'Now hold it like this,' you say. His arm is as stiff as a crane and the rod looks like a flagstaff in his hands.

'Let the float go down. Let some line out ... no, old chap, no Smith ... out! Let it out! The other way. No, don't lift it out of the water to see what's happening ... look ... STRIKE!'

At the word 'Strike' dear old Smith acts like a bemused robot who knows that it is all nothing to do with him. He gives a dramatic jump, bounds to his feet, hops on one leg and whips up the rod like a man saving the game. Float, hook, weights and cast all bind themselves into a tree whose branches, you were sure, began at a safe height.

Two hours later his instant success still hasn't come, and he's reading the *Sunday Times* colour section and thinking about changing his car.

Luckily you have been catching fish which, in such circumstances, is an unusual thing. Wouldn't do to have a bad day yourself when you desperately need to show Smith that there are fish swimming in the river.

By now you are aware of being nothing more than an angling public relations officer. So you make a great show with the landing net over that one pound bream you take. You say ... 'got one!' You say it loudly. And you grin. He looks up from the picture of the Super Saloon and says 'Umm' or 'Aha' or 'Oh yes?'. He might, if he's a sensitive Smith, add 'Well done'.

The most extreme remedies are now called for. The rain is making inroads into the newspaper and Smith is standing up. He's starting to look around helplessly. He's smoking a lot of cigarettes. He needs instant success now, this minute.

Drag him off to the cattle-dip shallows then, where a myriad gudgeon will go for a myriad gentles all day and never tire. Instant success? Well, here it is. Drag him to it. Guide his arm, swing out the rod, pull the line off his reel ... there ... there ... there

He's suddenly standing beside you with a little speckled sliver of a thing dancing away in front of his nose.

'What is it ... a sprat?' he asks, blinking at its struggles. 'Not very big, is it?'

The gudgeon gives a reproachful squeak, and at this point, with the rain setting in, you give up. Or maybe you don't give up. But Smith does. He's given up from the moment he found that learning to fish requires a certain amount of study.

In later weeks you won't find him there whenever you lean over the garden fence to borrow his lawn mower. It isn't likely to be anything you said, it is just that he doesn't want any more invitations to river banks.

Quite the oddest aspect of this is that he feels the need to keep out of sight because he truly believes that you are waiting to pounce, that you are bursting to get him to those river banks again.

Once Smith knows that you no longer want to do more than borrow his mower, it is a return to the friendly, sensible relationship arranged by nature for anglers and non-anglers. He is back in the ranks of those who rattle out the old remarks like 'Caught anything, apart from a cold?' and 'Got anything for the cat?' He's also back among those who make that hoary gesture in which both hands are employed to give the traditional angler's lie (rarely attempted by anglers) about the size of the 'one that got away .. ha ... ha.'

As I said, beware. Better still, don't bother. Such a failure is a nasty blow. It can even make you have doubts. Too much of Smith and you could be wondering whether there really is anything in the 'game' after all.

18. Walton's Walks

As Fisherman walked with Falconer and Hunter on that fine May morning when a legend and literature was born, I wonder if he knew that he was an exceedingly lucky man? Indeed, I'll bet that no such luck has ever since been with the talkative angler.

What I always ask is, why didn't he bore the pants off them? Granted that Izaak Walton gave Fisherman a truly marvellous gift of the gab. Granted that in the days when anglers were compleat rather than complete there was lots of healthy walking to do, and talking passed the time. But unless his two companions were different beings from their like today, three hundred years or so later, then I cannot understand why they tolerated him and seemed to enjoy it.

Of course the Falconer did drop out of it all pretty quickly, didn't he? Nipped round a park wall and got away. Probably told his friends to watch out for a talkative fellow puffing up Tottenham Hill and be ready to hide till he passed.

But the Hunter was... well... hooked, if you like. Even converted. And that's amazing. Well, I mean, have you ever tried to tell a hunting man about any sport unconnected with horse or hound? I have. And it doesn't work. Few of them want to divide their attention between fox and fly – and as for suggesting that they divide it between fox and maggots, or fox and a bit of soggy breadcrust... that's as difficult as expecting them to buy a ticket for the Hunt Saboteurs' annual ball.

The hunting men I've known have rarely been of the sort who inspired Oscar Wilde to produce that maddeningly misquoted and worn-out line about the unspeakable and the uneatable. Most of them in fact have had the nature of Venator, which was civilised and seemingly malleable. Unlike Walton's hunter however, their spirit of enquiry was only good manners. To sadly quote another immortal quote (far more outrageous than Wilde's) my hunting friends are all half way to believing that the person at the other end of the line, if not quite a fool, is certainly to be pitied.

I'd walk with Walton tomorrow if I could, and who wouldn't? As this is not possible, and all the modern-day giants of angling are fully booked by hordes of fans, I have to make do with such walks and talks as I find. The last one I took was not with Venator or Auceps. It was with a species unknown to Walton, called Motorist.

Actually I had seen this chap ambling around on the quietest of hired hacks so, by stretching things a bit, I reckoned he qualified as Venator. I was carrying rods and heading for a trout stream. He was carrying string gloves and walking from where he had parked his vintage car to a pub with a fruit machine. We talked about fishing. At least, I talked about fishing. But all the attempts I made to give him a glimpse into the world of trout and fly scarcely inspired anything at all. His chief interest was in the incredible fact that I was actually prepared to spend all day at it.

'What all day? All day d'you say? Wouldn't do for me old man, wouldn't have the patience.'

So we stopped talking about fishing and talked about vintage cars. At least, he talked about vintage cars. I was glad when he turned off for his bitter and the fruit machine. I was not so glad to spy the moral which is concealed in the fact that I was bored by vintage cars. Anyway, even a Walton couldn't have done anything with him.

The more naive among us might imagine that the nearest you can get to a Waltonian walk these days is with another angler as a companion, and forget about your Venators and your Auceps and your Motorists. What a pity Walton himself didn't think of the idea, but perhaps he knew the dangers. It may be alright to tack on a bit of Cotton or a bit of Venables just to compleat the angler, but the truth is that if he'd introduced another piscator face to face with the one who walked up Tottenham Hill, there'd have been a mighty row.

Unless you are very young or very new to fishing you do not discuss it all the time. You may walk with an angler companion in May or on any other morn and your talk might, indeed must, be spiced with fishing. But make it general, even vague, make it poetic if you like... and above all make it uncontroversial. At least, do that if you have in mind something of the calm dignity that existed on Walton's walks.

The trouble, as Walton's critics proved, is that other people have their own ideas. This is the most unfair fact of life I know. How much harmony there would be if they would only accept one's own views. Especially when one has strong views... as I have about the way to use a reel.

It was this that ruined the last piscator-to-piscator chat I had. The day was clear, the turf felt like sheepskin and the old pipe had declared a bonus of sweetness. My crusade on reels had to be launched against these because it is the only original practical contribution I feel able to make to the art of angling.

If I'm to be remembered for anything, I'm determined it shall be as the man who made anglers put their reels the right way round. At the moment I think I am my only disciple. Everyone else in the world seems to be in deep, black error.

All the other anglers in the world have their reel handles facing outwards, on the off-side of the rod. This means that they have to be turned with the right hand.

And as most of the anglers in the world are right handed, and the right hand is needed to hold the rod, this position for the reel is obviously ludicrous.

My companion on this occasion did not think it was ludicrous. Like everyone else he has for years preferred to switch his rod to his left hand in order to get the right free for reeling in. His reason is as idiotic as everyone else's: merely that he's 'got used to it that way'. What a fearful burden of conscience the writers of angling textbooks and guides to young fishermen must carry!

After a good twenty minutes of this chat and all my excellently voiced arguments being turned against the uncompromising 'It's what I've always done', we began to get quite testy with each other. I even reached the stage of pointing out that one day, when he actually hooked a big fish, he'd be in trouble. Some of the big barbel I know would just love to catch him changing his rod from one hand to the other.

At that point the turf seemed to lose its soft resilience, and my pipe got blocked by a gooey mess of saliva and tobacco shreds. Which served me right I suppose. However, Walton would have failed here too, despite his persuasive power.

On reflection I think I was a little hasty in dismissing old Auceps from the picture. I bring back that elusive falconer now, with apologies. One of his kind has been the fittest of companions for the walk and talk. And this one was not a crashing failure, though perhaps its real effect was unsuspected.

My falconer looked like a Romany and moved as if he was always one step away from the game-keeper. He was lithe and tall with shiny black eyes, black hair and a black moustache. At the time he was training a Goshawk which had arrived in a crate at London Airport and I remember the nature of its entry into this country because the letter saying when the bird was due had baffled us. A few days before the plane landed the falconer and I traversed half the metropolis trying to find someone who could read Norwegian.

After being so helpful (I found the translator ... it cost a pound) the falconer invited me to come into his idea of eternal bliss. We ran like deer (at least, he did) through a large number of woods and heathlands while his Gos swung ahead, low and fast, looking for rabbits.

I achieved a lot of superficial knowledge about falconry, which is a sport demanding far greater true patience than even a carp fisher could know. After a time I even got used to seeing him feeding the hawks from a bloodstained bag hanging round his waist and filled with entrails and the odd cockerel's head. When the Gos was hooded and quiet we talked, by the light of oil lamps I remember.

He let me have my head when the talk moved first to country sports generally and then to fishing in particular.

I flatter myself that under the stimulus of lamplight and quiet I rose to great heights in my praise of water and fish.

I can see him now, listening patiently, the light moving in his deep eyes as he bent over the tasselled buckskin gauntlet he was making. Yet sometimes I fancied that his eyes were becoming as hooded as his hawk's, though it may have been merely a wick burning low muffling the room with shadows.

I confess that later I gave up the role of Piscator – from choice and not from desperation at getting nowhere with conversion. It happened somewhere among trees when the newly trained Gos floated away and the invisible link between it and the falconer collapsed suddenly. Rapport laboriously built up, dissolved and became merely air between the outstretched hand and long fading wingbeats.

In the falconer's eye was pain. I saw it there. In his soul was pain. We beat the woodland until late evening. He called and called until the trees huddled together in bulk and starlight rested coldly upon their crowns.

There was some glow within for me too when we sighted the Gos, a sulking blob on a high branch. And I shared some of the joy when the falconer, after camping all night under the tree, made the triumphal recapture in the early morning. I watched him swing the feathered lure on the end of its string for two hours.

He told me once that the stoop of the Peregrine is even more spectacular than the Goshawk's dive bombing. I never found out. Walton didn't either, as far as I know. But I doubt if he regretted it.

19. One In The Eye With A Wet Myth

The landlord eyed me happily as I swam through the door. Outside, the river meadows were merely foundations for a wall of water. The rain was so heavy that it had weighed down my rod. It was also endless rain – a remarkably wet and hissing endlessness. So I'd given up, and gone in like a man with a tidal wave after him. Then I dragged a long, wet, miserable trail to the bar.

Just as I was considering that the double was a laughably small droplet to set against the ocean outside, the jovial chap brushed an index finger over his moustache, gave a little tug at some distinguished stripes knotted round his neck, and bustled up. Then he came out with that classic statement. It made me cringe.

You know what it was, of course. Everyone who fishes knows it. The drawback is that those who don't know a centrepin from a butt-ring are very much aware that it is the thing to say.

'Nice drop of rain sir, they tell me it's good for the fishing... makes 'em bite'.

Ouch! Well, what do you say? What can you say?

Slowly I removed a sodden Scottish fishing hat which had been well and truly spayed. Equally slowly I rolled back a cold and clammy shirt cuff...

And I asked him to have one with me. He said he didn't mind if he did and ducked in a professional manner over a pale ale.

My offer of a drink was a cunning move to change the subject. Nothing would have made me leave that pub until the rain slackened sufficiently for me to reach my car and

One In The Eye With A Wet Myth

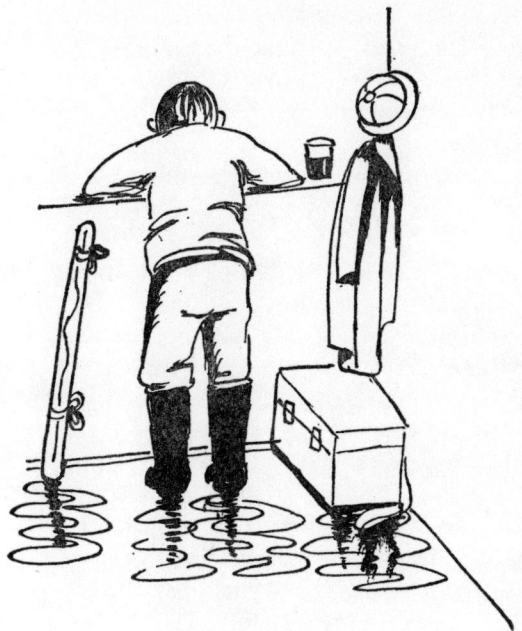

The Wet Myth

go home. And in an early morning moment of mad optimism I'd left the car a mile away. If I had to stay in the pub, then I wasn't going to get involved in talk about fishing with a man who reckoned I was always praying for rain.

It didn't work. It never does. He went on so fast to talk about 'biting' and how a 'good drop of rain' made all the big ones 'come up', that it made you think he'd been starved of conversation for a dozen wet seasons through.

The hissing outside got turned down a decibel or two, and changed into a dismal slurp against the shaking sash windows. The landlord went on talking and looking as if he might lose me at any minute when I rushed back to the river so as not to lose the joy of pulling out all the big ones which had come up in the rain.

'We get lots of anglers here,' he said. I looked round the bar.

In one corner was a cat. In another corner was a travelling salesman who had climbed out of a car which had a monster cigarette screwed to the roof. Not another angler did I see. Not even a sign that anglers had ever been there... unless the travelling salesman had a crafty rod stowed away somewhere. Perhaps he had it in the monster cigarette.

The landlord seemed to get the message. 'They're all out on the river now' he said. Seeing me nod he added, 'I expect they will be in later on when it clears'.

For a giddy moment I began to see things all jumbled up, and I was only on my second double too. Did the man mean that all the anglers of this strange region would be in when the sun shone, in some crazy retreat from the onset of deadly dryness? I almost felt I was missing something. But I swallowed, and the feeling passed.

Tolerant men will know that the landlord's rain-is-beloved-of-anglers line was used, as it always is, as a conversational opening – a pleasant gesture made in deference to your wholly incomprehensible pastime.

It's no use explaining that the idea is only partially true; that floodgates crumbling in the sky lead to a gumming-up of the mechanics of angling; that only afterwards it might be a blessing... low water... etc., etc. The truth is that he doesn't want to know. He is not interested in discovering that anglers don't mind the occasional sprinkle or that fishing is, first and foremost, supposed to be a pleasure. To be even more blunt, he isn't particularly interested in angling at all, but it would never do for him to show this.

I know a non-angling landlord at a riverside pub is a terrible thing, almost an insult to the law of nature, but there are more of them about than you like to think. They lurk among pewter and dark oak; they have photographs taken of themselves beaming under glass-cased specimens while some well-known angling face cranes round their shoulders.

All this is innocent though. After all what is there really wrong in being a sort of ex officio member of the brotherhood of the angle? And if you stop short at the angle, well, you make up for it by selling thin ties with a design of crossed pike bungs on them.

And so it goes with the fishy conversation. To take him up on his little pleasantries would be cruel. It would also bore him. And one bored customer is enough for any pub.

But hold on... he was rising again. 'What do you catch here, sir?' he asked, as I was watching the travelling salesman take out a book with an elastic band on it and wipe the rainwater off with a monogrammed company handkerchief.

'The odd trout, sometimes a grayling' I said.

'Is the rain good for them too?'

'Well...'

I was saved from saying what I thought by the landlord's wife who called from some inner chamber and emerged in front of the shout. She had a sulky look. It grew into an almost hostile look as she saw my dripping waders and the dripping waterproof jacket which I had removed and hung on a chromium hat rack. The garment was now suspended over a puddle.

'The gentleman's been fishing Vera'.

Vera, who shouldn't have been at a riverside pub either, gave a ghastly grin which scarcely stretched her vermilion lipstick. As she moved with her husband through a curtain that separated the two bars I heard her mutter something about 'Fishing! He must be mad.'

When he came back alone he was obviously wondering if I'd heard. Flicking a jovial look behind him at the curtain, he murmured: 'I thought of taking it up once. The wife wouldn't have it. Said it was too messy and I'd keep coming home with a cold'.

He looked very man-to-man when he said that. He also indicated that he'd told Vera that anglers don't mind mud and that they glory in rain.

I was beginning to feel sorry for him and even more sorry for myself. The rain was still sucking at the windows but I made those small preparatory movements recognised in pubs as the working-up to the goodbye. But just then the door banged open. Loudly. Equally loudly, it was banged shut.

There, gasping and glistening as I had been, was another refugee from the river. He was short and youngish and red-faced. He was also more fed up than I had been; the reason was that he was more soaked. He'd gone up river in nothing but heavy tweed and the stuff had absorbed so much water that his trail, as he lumbered past me to the bar, looked like a fishable tributary.

The landlord left me and put on a new proud smile of welcome, justified by having two anglers in one slack day.

'Hello, sir, good fishing?'

'What!' said the wet young man.

The landlord looked slightly disturbed. 'They say rain's good for the fish' he said.

'Look, do me a favour and don't be so bloody silly man. Just get me a drink.'

At this loud and jarring note the travelling salesman looked up from his book with the rubber band attached. The cat blinked and, as the rain itself seemed suddenly to pause in amazement, you could just hear the faint laughter from the spirits of intolerant fishermen down long centuries of repression.

The landlord smiled a dreadful smile and came back to me and his pale ale. He made a crestfallen wiping motion across the bar and in a low voice told me: 'We get all types in here sir, but it's nice to meet you. I can always spot a real angler.'

My cheerful 'goodbye' was the mouthing of a hypocrite. But his answering farewell was made in understanding from one exponent of angling lore to another.

20. On The Other Side

If the grass is always greener on the other side of the fence it is positively a blazing, technicoloured, siren-like green on the other side of the river.

George knows this. He does more than just know. He acts accordingly... usually. George has great wisdom and I learn from him.

When George approaches a river which he hasn't fished before, he mentally tosses a coin. Sometimes he actually does toss a coin. But more often he does an eeny meeny minee mow in his mind while lighting a reflective cigarette. If it comes down 'heads' – and heads is the left bank – then he fishes on the right bank. He does the same thing with 'mow', nodding and full of resolution.

It is not cussedness nor eccentricity (well, maybe tossing a coin is just a bit odd): it is, in fact, based on a strong awareness of the strangeness and unfairness of things. Not, I must say, that it ever seems to do him much good. After all, you can play the same trick with pockets.

Pockets are as sly and misleading as river banks. Say you are in a rush to go somewhere and an article you need is in a coat hanging up. It may be your car keys, your season ticket, your income tax return or your wallet. You are in a rush so you plunge your hand into a pocket.

Never. But absolutely never, is the thing in the pocket you first try. Basic law of life. It is always in the other one. Or, at least nine times out of ten it is in the other pocket.

Or maybe it isn't in any pocket at all, but under the piano or in the bathroom cabinet. Still, that doesn't count. If it is in the garment at all it is in the other pocket. Or if you are cursed with a multitude of pockets it is in the last one you come to.

Now, you say to yourself, by every scientific law I like to think of, whether it comes from science or not, I should get a first time win if I check myself.

So you do. You watch your hand dashing to pocket A and you say... Aha... then you get a mind-grip on the hand, pull it back and, with a smirk, sink it into pocket B instead.

Nine times out of ten again, the damned thing is in pocket A. Frustrating. Uncanny.

The same thing happens with George, and with me, and probably with you. Only it is worse with river banks. You can't dart about between them because they have the well-known characteristic of being separated by water... often deep, often wide. And, if you plump for the left hand bank, say, you have usually gone the whole hog and walked so far along it that it is half a day's trek back to the only crossing point. So when it turns out to be the worst bank you ever trod, you lump it and grind your teeth. Which doesn't do anything to improve the fishing.

Perhaps this is why, when fishing happily on your own bank (having been lucky on your one time out of ten), a socking great leger weight comes soaring over from somewhere opposite and lands on your float.

The chap who threw it might apologise. And you might understand. But he rarely does... and so you don't. If he thinks the grass is greener where you are then you want to keep it to yourself, so he can fiddle about on his brown arid stubble till kingdom come, and you tell him so.

George never casts leger weights into other people's green pastures. He's a sportsman. When he finds the colour's gone against him he sinks into a sort of resignation. He humps himself down, grumbles low for hours and finally lapses into a mental torpor.

Me... I cast the leger weight. Though I do try to make sure it doesn't hit anyone. I'm a rebel I think. I fight uncanny forces.

If anyone doubts that they are uncanny then let him pause and think about it. Why, for instance, is the wind always blowing in your face? See what I mean? If it is your face it is blowing from the opposite bank. Why are all the nice curves full of fishy eddies absent on your side and present in abundance on the other side? And those clear runs between weed – aren't they always over there, while all you have here is the weed, in great unbroken sheets.

'Today', says the knowledgeable bankside-strolling local expert, 'today you should be fishing in Paradise Hole' (or 'Tom's Glide', 'The Mill Pool' or all the others).

'Really?' you say, after being without a bite for countless hours. You are interested. Very. Where is Paradise Hole? Let me get to it.

'Full of fish on a day like this. You can't go wrong', he says.

'Really', you say again... drooling.

'I can tell you that conditions are just right for Paradise Hole'.

You ask him to lead the way. Point it out. Tell me. You are almost shrieking.

'Well you are on the wrong bank,' he says. 'It's a good mile and a half round by the bridge.'

So you forget Paradise Hole where the water dives to eight feet and continue to fish with the wind in your face, pulling out masses of weed from eighteen inches of ooze that runs along your side to the next county. Or if you are like George you do.

More robust characters stride off again along the despised home bank to find a better swim. Or perhaps they are looking for stepping stones. Or the appearance of a friendly boatman. But friendly boatmen are as invisible as stepping stones these days. They are as rare as fish from banks you have lost all faith in.

This raises a deep, deep truth about fishing. Something to be whispered only to the deserving. Something worth a box of flies a year or a season's supply of gentles.

If you want to have success, if you want to catch fish... then you must be full of anticipation. You must see the float as perpetually ready to dive away. You must get a creeping sensation on your neck when the leger swings round to that certain spot. You must thrill inside when the fly trips innocently over that certain ripple of water.

If you see the float as a ridiculous and uninspired piece

of painted uselessness, or catch your arm aching with hopeless casting; if your leger looks like so much dead weight catching weed, then it's all up with you.

And if you let the bank get you down, and lose all faith, then you will sink into despair. Like George. But to give George credit, he did once try.

We were watching a fellow on the other bank. He was like a metronome. I could see him even though I was hiding behind a big bush, lest the non-existent fish in my swim should be disturbed. The man was fishing from a point that jutted out into the river and commanded a fine swim on the inside of a bend. The river was quite wide but I saw the movements as he cast. So did George. Almost instantly the man opposite was in to a fish, a good heavy one. George and I sucked in our breaths.

Cast (click)... strike (click)... cast (click)... strike... that's how it seemed to go. It got on my nerves. It got on George's nerves too. He had one tiny dace that had not grown old enough to learn about river geography: I had an older gudgeon who had long ago forgotten about river geography.

That's all we had. And here was this chap sitting among his greenery on the other bank, pulling them out monotonously. We saw them flashing in his landing net. They were big and fat with fine red fins beckoning us.

It was too much for George. He growled and collected his tackle. 'Going to try the other bank,' he said. I watched him stump off and marvelled at this. What he was doing was unique.

Then followed a long wait. I stayed where I was. The man opposite stayed where he was and went on catching fish. Minutes passed. Then more minutes.

After a long time I stood up and stared across the river for some sign of my friend. In the distance I saw a twinkle.

Shading my eyes I stared harder at the opposite bank and saw that the twinkle some hundreds of yards upstream of me was ... George's feet.

Behind the feet was George sitting on the ground. He was wringing out wet socks. Obviously he had tried to ford the river.

Finally I saw George get to his feet and walk along the

bank so bravely gained towards the man who was catching fish. George came in triumph, with his waders full of wetness and his trousers slopping.

The man went on catching fish.

George came closer. He saw me and waved across the river. His rod, still made up and ready to go, waggled gaily.

The man stopped catching fish. He stopped because he had seen George.

I heard them talking. The man produced a card from his pocket and showed it to George. 'I hope you don't intend fishing on this bank,' he said. 'This is private,' he said.

For a moment George crouched like a churl with a cudgel. Then he wilted. I watched him walk wetly back the way he'd come. It was a long way back... to that bridge.

Know ye, that puny men can't defeat the fates.

21. Monster in Weak Tea
(from *Angling*, August 1968)

In angling there are many things I'm not sure about. I hope this will always be the case. But one thing I do know and can declare it with absolutely no doubt at all: that large, deep sand or ballast pits, which are still being worked, have been put into the world with the purpose of splitting anglers' souls and drowning their spirits. They are there, I'm convinced, to wash your ego into the ooze and to offer times of tribulation.

When you have had a good day on some delectable stream, or couldn't go wrong on one of those delightful ponds fringed with roots and lilies, then you are lulled into believing that mastery has come to your rod. On the next time out you carry your confidence elsewhere... to the pit perhaps. Then you're for it. Drawn down and flailed by the deadness of the water, you emerge tired, chastened, drained. You are ready to throw away the rods and take up golf.

What's that? You're not? You know a sandpit, or a gravel pit, where you'd choose to fish on the last day of your life? Well, so you say, and I don't believe it.

I've had a lot to do with pits when coarse fishing. Enough to know that the ones I fished in the past and, the Lord help me, the ones I fish now, are the same as those everybody else fishes. I always remember one such place with the same feelings you get when visiting the dentist. This pit, they told me, was in the process of becoming the finest roach water in the south of England. Men dedicated their lives to this end and compiled a vast book of rules to support them. If you put a foot out of line when angling there you were hanged, drawn and quartered... then minced up into groundbait.

Still, all this didn't help at all. The latest news I have (gathered from a safe distance) is that the place is still far from being the finest roach water in the south of England – despite an awful lot of groundbait.

So my mind has not been changed. My pits, and everybody else's pits, are merely vast hosts to each nasty nor'-easter that happens to be passing. This is easily proved, because they are always covered with seagulls who mistake them for the North Atlantic.

In the pit lives an evil thing called the thermocline which, some unscientific people still don't know (despite all the books), has to do with an area of dead water you must avoid. Actually it is a little more complicated than this (read the books), but it doesn't matter. In the pits you can play hunt-the-thermocline all day if you like, only to discover at the end that the thing is your own shadow... present wherever you sit.

On the other hand, should you have underwater springs, the thermocline may not really exist at all . . . like the fish.

The really cunning fact about pits, though, is that while the water always looks like weak tea, while the banks change their shape from day to day and tend to cave-in without warning just as you sit down – the area has the appearance of some strange amoeba living on shingle – they still somehow contrive to look inviting.

Aha... that is the lure! As a flycatcher plant must look beautiful to the fly, so the pit dresses itself up and uses the angler's own innate naivety against him.

An angler wants to like the place in which he fishes. He wants to feel excitement rising as he tears at the flap of his rodbag and aches to cast his float into a certain patch of water which almost smells of carp or tench or what have you. The pit knows these things. It gives a devilish twitch way down in its thermocline. And waits.

'Mmmm' you say, contentedly, resting your landing net on the Sunday immobility of a caterpillar digger... 'water looks good today'. The digger sits in a blankness of hot metal. Nylon slides through warm rings.

110 *Fishing Without Tears*

The thermocline goes on waiting.

Of course the water looks good. It is like the proverbial millpond. It is even a gentle green, and not brown. Over the placid surface come deep sporty sploshes, pinpricks of bubbles and spreading rings wherever you look. You feel happy inside and itching to get down there. Even the odd wispy sapling – planted in advance of the day when the river authority, and your club, will take over completely from the ballast company – looks like a shady forest caressing the water's edge.

Down you go, over the hollow concave slopes that lead to the spot you select. Pipe smoke goes straight upward and the sun smiles. The fishy rings are still spinning.

It is only after your float has pressed into the 22 feet of water under the bank that the first faint breeze appears. You say 'Mmmm' again and enjoy the coolness because the sun is rather hot. The breeze grows stronger. At first you don't notice, being occupied with landing the first struggling roachling and finding another biting already, almost certainly a pounder. It isn't. But this is to be a good day.

Down in the thermocline some secret signal is given and the jaws of the pit begin to close.

You find you can't light your pipe with one match any more. As the flame is shielded in cupped hands there comes a lapping sound against your feet. Looking down you see your line has grown an expanding belly.

This time primitive reflexes extract a 'Damn!' from you, instead of a 'Mmmm'. Yet, observing that the breeze is blowing in your face you come over all knowledgeable. Fish in the teeth of the wind is what the best books say... because of the thermocline and so on. Fortunate you are to have a bit of a breeze. You'll catch fish while all those other chaps are still hunting for windless swims.

Sad, deluded, pompous fellow! By the time you start wondering if it might be best to switch to the leger and sink the rod-tip one foot under, the jaws of the pit have slammed heavily shut.

Now there's a dance of joy down in the thermocline. Now the whole surface of the water is on the move. The first waves bring back the weak tea, the spineless saplings are gripped and shaken. Then the rollers break upon the shingle at your feet, building higher and higher, hissing over the bits of rusted iron and the last angler but one's fruit pie packet.

With the float jumping up and playing hide and seek or, if you acted fast, your dough bobbin lashing from side to side, the chances are that you will start thinking about golf. We all like a challenge, but some are so powerful that it might have been better to have finished painting the house or weeding the rockery.

'But what about the fish!' shouts the confirmed pitman. There's always a confirmed pitman about, the sort who takes his secret method to a secret spot in acres of alien weak tea every evening. What about the fish indeed. They, after all, are what you go for.

The pitman is right. Somewhere out there in the foaming main are fish of note. He knows. He's caught them. You know, because once there was that non-stop day which went down in your diary. And you have actually seen darn great convoys of carp on the move.

This, you must accept, is the foulest part of the whole foul confidence trick. If you think hard it will suddenly become clear that the day of note is never the one on which you are fishing. You might even recall that it was a day of note only for the reason that it rose up so unexpectedly among days that were forgotten through sheer blankness.

It is probably true that there are big fish in the pit, but for each reasonable specimen there are endless shoals of 'skimmer' bream, so pale and thin that they look as if they gave up the struggle to reach six ounces ages ago. For every two-pound perch there are infant hordes which can just about persuade themselves to do battle with a worm.

But the confirmed pitman remembers the time he 'broke up on something big', or the time Fred had his rod pulled in while replacing the stopper on his Thermos. Must have been a gargantuan trout.

As you gaze out into the breakers and see the swelling brew thickening, as you cling on to your hat with the hand you use for striking, you know these things we all believe. The pitman has the advantage because he offers hope. So you will certainly return, and I wish you luck!

Meanwhile, let the gale push you back to the car and, when your friends dig each other in the ribs and ask why you had such a bad day, look wise. Blame it on the wind. Or the temperature. Or barometric pressure.

Better still, blame it on the thermocline.

22. Of Charms and Fancies

When we lived in caves and knew that black was evil and darkness concealed dangers, and that white was good because daylight revealed dangers, there must have been any amount of charms and luck-bringers and magic. A lake-dweller with hardly a skin to his back might have had the basic thrills of angling, but more likely it was just his stomach talking. And, because his stomach often had to do a lot of talking, he needed magic.

As Mr Trog went fishing he snatched up whatever preceded the bent pin and whatever it was he used as a line before shambling off with the most important fishing article of all... a bit of carved wood or the sun-dried heart of a three toed thingummy.

When Mr Jones goes fishing it is not so easy to spot the bits of magic. For centuries anglers have been mixing strange things into their groundbait, but Mr Jones probably doesn't do that now... unless it be a crafty drop of pilchard oil when no-one is looking, or a secret diehard belief in oil of tar for tench.

I'm a great believer in crushed eggshells myself, but that's for a reason that is both scientific and logical of course. Of course.

Anglers' superstitions are endless and well catalogued. Some, we know, shudder when the wind is in the east (not only because there is some evidence that this is worth shuddering at) and put their rods away. Others would never dream of wetting their keep nets until the first fish is taken. Some even refuse to make up their landing nets until a fish is taken – and the cure for that is a terrible one.

Of Charms and Fancies

Sadly, this isn't real magic. The real stuff isn't easy to find, yet you never know. Last Spring I thought I was on to something quite primeval. I was doing a new season's walk along a stream that I fully intended to flog into submission later when there was this fellow just in front. On his knees he was, muttering over a charm and with his rod stuck upright in the ground beside him on the buttspike.

His hands were over his face. It was a noteworthy obeisance and obviously significant as the sun was hot upon the stream and there was a crying need to do something because the trout were certainly wearing dark glasses. I stood reverently behind him and said nothing. It was a little like feeling oneself an atheist carpenter in a cathedral pew.

But I was glad I didn't say anything like... well... 'is it working?' or 'try facing the other way'. I was glad I remained silent because this man suddenly started to let out small swear words and hisses through his teeth. And when he took his cupped hands away from his face it was clear that an Iron Blue Dun on 4X had gone beyond the barb into a nostril.

A psychiatrist friend of mine thinks there's something interesting in the angler whose first act on arrival at a selected swim is to crush and tear-up every piece of bankside vegetation in front of him. Just watch next time. They do it with such single-mindedness that you might wonder if it isn't some vestigial instinct, like a dog turning round and round before lying down.

Of Charms and Fancies

And what about the peculiar effect of pike? Here's a man who has caught one. What does he do? His eyes flash, he growls in his throat and bashes the pike's head. Real stone-age stuff... trampling fear under foot and gaining strength from ritual slaughter.

In case anyone thinks I am free from all this then I must tell him that I thought so too. Then I lost my disgorger.

Strange, about this disgorger. I bought it around fifteen years ago for sevenpence and the only fact I am sure of in this life is that it is the best disgorger ever made.

I have never seen a disgorger like it. It is of solid metal with a generous hole at the business end. None of your snapping plastic or bits of bent wire with useless forked ends, or lightly chromed things that won't slip over an eyed hook and seem made only to tear the binding of ready-tied hooks.

This is the undoubted king of disgorgers and, quite seriously, I have never fished, not even for half an hour, without knowing that it was handy. I remember the shop where I bought it, the man who served me – he was a cobbler who fished when not cobbling – and all the operations I have conducted with its aid.

Down a thousand gasping throats by a thousand rivers it has gone. It has rattled past the minute teeth of trout, buried itself in the throat grinders of chub and been used in demonstrations for those who have yet to learn the knack of pushing and turning.

Until I lost the disgorger I had never considered it as a talisman. But the shock was great. After every pocket in every disreputable jacket I possess had been searched and searched again; after the house had been ransacked, the car dismembered, I began to feel distraught and go around with a white face.

What made things worse was that I had lost it after a week's intensive fishing on at least two rivers apart from my usual territory, three lakes and an ornamental lily pond. And as I had not needed a disgorger at any time (No... they had been properly hooked) and had been misled by a pencil in my pocket, the chances of finding it seemed remote.

I made a backtrack hunt. It failed. So I tried to forget.

Once I even thought about buying a replacement, but the idea felt like slitting the throat of my dog.

On the first time out when disgorger-less I might just as well have been fishing with no bait. I caught nothing. What is more to the point... I expected to catch nothing.

On the second time out I found a long glide which was familiar and where the grayling were just popping out all over. The fourth one I took came after a delayed strike – caused when being taken off guard as I was lighting my pipe with one hand and trying to sight the float over a flaming match.

The fish had the hook just too far down for the fingers. So I swivelled round and grabbed the disgorger. It took at least a second for me to recall that I'd lost the thing a fortnight ago.

This, I prefer to think, was magic. A talisman come home to roost. The disgorger was stuck in the ground beside my seat-basket as though it had dropped from the sky, and the rational explanation, though clear, is of no interest to me whatsoever.

All right. It is only a disgorger after all. But, as I don't bash pike or worry overmuch about east winds, I feel I am entitled to some indulgence.

23. Beauty—I Tell You It's Torture!

They say all seasons are fine by the water. Sometimes they may be right. But I reckon it all depends on your blood circulation. When you're feeling poetic about the fishing scene you should wash it down with a hot toddy, because pure torture is just round the corner.

Angling beauty is all right most of the time. There were mornings once when a small lake was draped in a flow of rising mist that peeled back at the corners and slid away above the trees. The mist left a bright new water surface, puckered with tench bubbles, yet seeming unbroken in the stillness.

To get down to this lake you used good fortune and crossed fingers. The paths between fern and nettle, rhododendron and chestnut trees, turned round upon themselves. Only one path led to the water and the feeling was that if you didn't find it quickly those precious hours, before the sun struck too hard upon the world, would be lost, and the big tench would go to sulk among the lilies.

Always in this place there was a heron. A gaunt and grey heron. Always there. Always gaunt. He would be standing where the lake ran out into a trickle of a brooklet that twisted away on a bed laid by the dead leaves of centuries. As I arrived the heron would mutter and sigh between bony, humped shoulders. Then he would lurch away into the rising mist, which disembodied him. Only a grey head and one extended leg blew upwards through the trees. His last, lost wingflaps left a solitude so absolute that my ears hummed.

So I would stumble quickly over the bank to tackle up.

The disturbed mud smelled of peat and gaslighter fuel. The ground was gripped by the half-exposed roots of pines.

There, at last, was the bright tip of the float cocked, primed and piercing – ready to do all its trembling and lifting and jerking and running away deep down where mighty things move unseen.

Where was that lake? It existed. It exists still, I hear. But nobody need ask where it is because it belongs to everyone. All anglers have it for themselves.

It is many years since I fished there. In fact I doubt if I shall ever fish there again. Yet, if I were to play that psychological parlour game of word association and someone rapped out 'Fishing'... I know I would think of that lake with its heron and the tree roots worn smooth.

But I don't think of my lake when summer has slipped away and become bonfires. With Autumn there's a new nostalgia. As the season of brass aproaches and leaves lie like dead friends I suppose I think first of the river.

The wind sandpapers the face and a mental picture of the river fills the shortening days. Here is the heavy flow that has borne down the weed and borne up the spirits of the fish. Now roach spring blood red and hard at the sunken breadcrust which is at last unchallenged by the extravagant supply of natural food. Now the last chattering picnickers are brushing the crumbs from tartan travelling rugs. Now the transistors are dying in droves.

Autumn by my river is a seat in the crisp reeds and feet in inches of water that rise from summer level and lap the lip of the bank. The days grow vitals of steel and the moorhen moves all uncovered, robins come more boldly at the maggot tin – and all who fish are there to fish.

These harsher months on Winter's border are new life to the man who fishes. It is life as powerful in its way as the traditional emergence of Spring. At this time the poets are still there, and with justification. It is as if a fat man has grown lean.. The cloying days of insect hum and lushness are sloughed off like obesity under a rigorous diet. The angler who bursts from such a chrysalis takes the air with nostrils flared and scenting power sharpened.

Forgotten the tench and the heron, never remembered the delicate dangle with the fly and whispy rod – here is alertness put on with extra clothing.

This is the time for the slashing strike of the hunter who gives a lusty bellow as the rod plunges and line whines away into the water like taut piano wire... with a piano on the end.

Woodsmoke and Autumn roach, Spring and the first trout – are real yet unreal. They are things built on a framework of themselves. The finished product is an emotion created from a formless rush of Autumns and Springs stretching back through the years.

Yet the guts of the matter is harder than this. Fishing cannot be a mere spread of aesthetic emotion, and the man who says it is does the art no service. For angling is sometimes pure misery. I said it was torture and I mean it. A pastime fashioned for fools.

Take a good look now at Winter, deep Winter by the river. It needs a man drunk with Summer to see it wholly as a symphony of bare trees waving through black and white, while crows fly above the rod to furious debates in speckled fields.

I am thinking now of the day I went to a sullen river when February sat hard on Sussex. I had a bag of sprats and the idea of fishing them sink and draw for monster pike.

If there is anyone who wants to mortify the flesh just for the hell of it, then I recommend baiting sprats on wire as the snow beats up all around and the hands grow as insensitive as treble hooks. With numbness crawling out of my boots and ice tinkling hard as I crunched through the mud, I searched that slug-coloured water from dead bay to dead bay, eddy to eddy.

The only moving thing on such a marble slab of a day, the only life either in or out of the water, was me. Not a pike did I sense, let alone feel.

Each stiff sprat rasped on the wire trace and looked at me in ghastly mockery. I felt I had a good tip for those who cooked up the labours of Hercules: first catch your pike, then you can go. And so I promised myself. The snow came thicker. Then it came whiter. Then I made another promise: first catch something, anything. Then get out of here fast.

When a crack appeared briefly in the cold around early afternoon I cursed my sprats and threw the remaining ones away. Then I did one or two stumbling runs up and down the bank and, when able to feel my fingers again, went in for a bit of frenzied demolition work. With a pair of shot-pliers I snapped off two hooks from my smallest treble. Ever tried to do this in the snow? It takes as much effort as climbing the Matterhorn or painting the Forth Bridge. But it was necessary. All I had was pike tackle.

At length I had a single hook. Wiping away the blood from my fingers, I tied the hook directly to the 10 lb. b.s. line. Then I pinched on one shot and baited with bread from a frozen sandwich.

Sinking down beside a bush that rattled in the wind like a chandelier loaded with broken glass, I dropped the tackle into a deep backwater and dredged away like a madman.

I didn't deserve to land a dace of half a pound or so... and I didn't land it. But at least I hooked it, and we were both extremely surprised. He came up like one who knows he should never have got out of bed.

I had no net of course (a gaff is hardly the thing for dace) and, having been too miserable and cold to strike properly, he wasn't well hooked anyway. As I pulled him up, sensing release from all this cold misery, he fell off with a baleful plonk and went back to bed.

That's it! I said. Quietly I'll confess that I was feeling just a little proud of my adaptability, but I had no heart to go on with the business of fishing. Denied the full warmth of a triumphal glow, I stuffed everything into my bag and floundered away.

Kindly thoughts about the poetry of Winter fishing did not begin until the river was only a fading blink out of the carriage window – and I discovered the blissful fact that British Rail had left the heating on.

24. Something For the Wall

Secret sin jumped out and hit me when a dingy room in my tottering cottage was finally redecorated. The redecoration surprised everyone, as the dinginess, spiced with a touch of damp, had seemed kind of traditional. The sin surprised nobody – except me.

When I looked around this room I liked the new brightness, but there was this gap in the decor. Something must go there, people said. Digby looked in to boast about some grayling he'd had, and said the same thing.

'A fish', I said... 'in a case... that's what we want'.

My wife came in and went out again looking grim and thoughtful at the same time. I do not have a fish in a glass case. That's the trouble.

This gap in a wall of books is the chimney breast. It stands out stark and white in matt finish. Once some Victorian had a picture of a dying warrior up there. After that, there's evidence from the 30s that somebody hung up a mirror dripping with shiny bits, curves and fan shapes.

Now it's virgin whiteness again the responsibility has had me thinking about joining one of these groups of specimen hunters which are the latest thing in angling. I think they give you a badge and a uniform and have drill nights twice a week. Once I met one sitting well back from the river bank and standing guard over a barbel he said was 14 lb. The fish was in the water waiting to be caught, and I asked why wasn't he trying to catch it.

He lit another cigarette and looked puzzled at my innocence. 'Waiting for my spotter, aren't I' he said.

It seems that, in the highest specimen groups, barbel

fishing is a team game. One man dangles the luncheon meat while the other lies on the bank downsteam wearing polaroid glasses and telling the one with the rod what's happening and where to let the leger roll. I wondered what happened when they landed a new record fish. Are the honours shared?

In any case, the qualifications for joining a group are rather high, so I've never been asked even to be a spotter. Perhaps that's why I have a blank bit of wall.

A doubt has hung about that not only might a fish look worse than a chromium-plated wall mirror, but that it would seem pretentious. My non-angling friends suggest the first and my angling friends hint at the second point. But I want a fish and, anyhow, it isn't their wall.

What happened was that I started the downward plunge to sin by dropping in to riverside pubs that specialise in cased fish... just for a quick drool into my beer of course. Fatal, that! Don't do it. For one thing it taints the beer.

A time comes when each of us must be honest. I've already admitted that I've never caught a glass-caser. More than that, though, is that I find it difficult to believe that I'm going to catch one in the future. At least... in the near future, before the room needs decorating again.

As it happens, this season I did have a fish that got me wondering. It was long and fat. It stayed in the net for half a day while I thought about knocking it on the head with a bank stick wrapped in a rod bag.

Fair enough, it was only a gudgeon. But it was a very mighty gudgeon. Close to the record (whatever that is these days) and I could have proved it if I'd had anything that weighed accurately in drachms.

My problem was that I happen to like gudgeon. I think they are splendidly gay and gallant toy barbel always ready to oblige. Have you noticed that when you take the hook out they look up at you in surprise – and squeak?

Yes, I'd kill a trout without a tremor, but the gudgeon is a friend. So I let this one go. Anyway, it must take an extremely proud and hard-necked man to hang a gudgeon on his wall, even if it is a mighty gudgeon and a small wall.

To be fair to myself, I have talked a lot about three particular trout, and was once actually clapped on the back over a roach. I've been happy with a lot of chub and delirious over two of them. And three seasons ago I released a giant villain of a pike while blokes around me said I shouldn't. 'That's worth setting up' they said. I preferred the warm and noble glow inside.

However, none of these fish were what I'd call a glass-caser, if only because you are expected to write the weight on the glass case. It's all right if you can put 3 lb. on your roach, but if you put 2 lb. people go around saying they got one too and didn't bother.

It's all problems in this game. Say you're out on the river tomorrow and, like me, have a space on a wall. By much skill and a bit of fortune you land something that makes you skip around in circles and think of fame. What would you do?

Many anglers would grab a witness or two, do a lot of careful weighing and a lot of careful photographing. Some might send this evidence, together with a scale or two, to some worthy journal which might, as a result, send them on a bumper holiday to Greenland or the Bahamas. But, assuming the fish isn't a new record, that's the end of the matter.

Those whose egos are bursting might tap the fish on the head and cart it home for a parade around those who will look and listen – and even around those who won't.

But, of course, most of us would put the fish back. We would do this for two reasons: in the first place it's being on the side of the angels and, in the second place, the cost of setting-up can be alarming. The real answer is simpler though... has anyone met any good taxidermists lately?

A taxidermist isn't a man anyone can put a finger on just like that. Once you could, but no longer. Turn up your diaries and address books and yellow pages, but Taxidermist will not pop up between Tailor and Taxman, however hard you look.

You only need problems like these, plus weakness of character, and you've got temptation. Add space on the wall and you've got sin. That's how I decided to buy a fish.

Round the corner, just off the village main street, I found

this little junk shop. It was the sort which hadn't yet made up its mind to tidy up and join the antiques boom. Long innocent looks through the window revealed to me a dusty-looking case with a far from dusty perch inside.

Let me say that the struggle lasted some time. On four occasions I passed that window and went on walking. I got used to peering quickly round a plant-stand, a hat rack and two deadly looking oil heaters – all without slackening pace. And over the days I discovered that the perch was bold and big and nicely barred. The case seemed quite presentable too, not so old-looking. With a bit of rubbing down it would pass.

I went in when the shop was empty. Alone in the place, which smelled of old tea leaves and woodworm, I picked up the case and found, with evil pleasure, that there was no name written on and even the weight had become illegible.

The thing was still in my hands when there came a shuffling sound behind me. A voice said 'Hullo again.. sir'.

It was the 'again' bit I didn't like. It nearly made me drop the case. But I recovered brilliantly. Snatching at my nerves I took a long, cool look at the stuffed perch as though seeing it for the first time and wondering how it got there. Deep inside I blasphemed and condemned the man for walking around his shop in carpet slippers.

'Not a bad fish that, is it sir... I caught it in Somerset just after the war'.

He caught it! Liar... I thought.

Somehow I managed to put the case back. It seemed to take a long time. Then I muttered something idiotic and grabbed the nearest object to hand.

'How much are these?' I asked, waving a pair of blackened antlers from Scotland, carved from the skull in 1880. The date was clear and there would be no false impressions.

'He said '7s 6d'... added quickly 'for the mounting'... and finished with 'Fifteen bob to you, sir'.

I fancied there was something smug and knowing about the way he shuffled over to his moneybox. When I got outside the world seemed made of eyes.

Only recently Digby was saying he had grown to like

the bare white wall over the fireplace. I gave him the antlers as a present and said he was the sort of bloke who'd tell people his grandfather had shot the monarch of the glen. He didn't even laugh, just looked thoughtful. I never did believe that I was the only sinner around.

25. It Was Something Big!

Nowadays I go sea fishing just once a year. I go to write things in a newspaper about Southern Television's sea fishing championship final which must be one of the happiest as well as the biggest events in the whole competition calendar. All the entrants are champion anglers and wholly dedicated. The rest of us, mere scribbling hangers-on, tend to keep the holiday spirit, but I've found that this can only be maintained before you get into the boats and after you climb out of them.

The competition waters tend to be somewhere dramatic off Orkney or Shetland – out there you feel like an explorer sent to find the weather forecast and never heard of again.

Your actual sea has a hostile tinge veering towards insane rage. Only cowards talk about it, the rest just walk a little taller afterwards. They do that even if they have spent the day dying with low moans.

The last time I was out there, with the Old Man of Hoy snarling at me and wave crests beating the higher clouds out of the way, I held a rod over the side with two pounds of lead swirling about somewhere below. The last thing in my mind was catching fish. The rod was just something to hold on to for the sake of balance. A fish would have been an embarrassment.

In fact on that occasion I was embarrassed only twice... first by something red, spikey and irate, whose name I didn't know, and then by a spur dog.

People said 'See that spike he's got above his tail?' 'Yes,' I said. 'Well,' they said, 'he'll drive it through your hand if you don't watch out.'

Something Big...

After dealing out death to the spur dog, accomplished with my survival-of-the-fittest bellow on a him-or-me basis, I spent the rest of the time cutting up soggy strips of mackerel with one hand and cutting a bottle of Scotch down to size with the other. Both hands were shaking.

I suppose I've never lost the strong feeling that the sea is not for fishing in. This is not a modern attitude. Modern anglers are advised to taste all joys, and in essence this means go trouting with a fly one day, breaming with paste the next and piking for monsters at the weekend.

Of course some people go out into the surf at least once in a while and battle with bass, or perhaps they stalk mullet in bleak estuaries, or sharpen up their biceps on conger, or merely relax among the flatties. They tell me these are pleasant things, particularly when one or other freshwater close season is causing them to twiddle their thumbs in boredom. Some even say that these are exciting things.

After hooking a skate that flapped up like an enraged bedstead ('Bit through the trace it did.. wire.. thick as a bike brake cable') a few trusting souls might undergo conversion. They might leave their reservoir rods to grow cobwebs, or their seat baskets to grow green mould. When that happens I don't mark them down as all-rounders; I say they've opted out of their species. They've joined the Titans.

Sea anglers are another breed of being, with Winter sports hats and huge wrists. They deal in a craft where everything is blatantly larger than life or, at least, larger than life as it is known to the paler men of rivers and streams.

You know that many of them have fine skill and knowledge, and when they say that you can face the oceans of the world armed only with a roach pole... well ... I don't mind believing them. But I don't lose sight of their image, which is fixed in my mind like a lighthouse.

It is pretty certain that the sea anglers I have known in the past were not representative of the breed, but they are still around. They roll heavily and buy hooks of the sort you feel should be used by butchers for hanging carcasses. And then they come back with the carcasses for the hanging.

They use great hunks of twisted nylon that put you in mind of rolls of telephone cable (the sort that goes underground). And the weights you see hanging from their mighty rods are hunks of metal that might just have cooled down after arrival from outer space.

Even those who don't fish like that still dabble with nasty things that make humble brandlings look like Queens of the May and the simple maggot look like a delicious dream of banquet nights.

On their tangle of hooks go convulsive animals in the nature of mutant centipedes, called ragworms or 'Rag'. They remind me of a fascinating description passed on by an Indian Army relative. He talked about crawling creatures on the walls out there.

'They climb up at night' he said... 'hooked legs dripping with poison. You turn on the light and pfffft! They spring at your face and if you don't brush them off the proper way you only drive the claws deeper into your skin'.

I've never actually seen ragworm do that, but I bet they could if they tried.

But for men of the sea there are many extremes in baits. There's the lugworm. For those happy game fishers who don't know about lugworm, I can best describe it as a sort of black slush encased in black slush – and likely to dissolve with a squelch and a pop as soon as the hook goes in.

Sea anglers never notice these things because they have their eyes on the far horizon. Their world, which is as far from the holidaymaker's handline and the child's shrimp net as it is from the trawling industry, consists of big boots and uncaring majesty.

These men do more than leave footprints of unearthly size in the early-morning sand. They make great casts from the beach, scramble gallantly over slippery rocks, or set out in overburdened boats that strike into the heart of gale warnings.

Actually, I took it seriously once – or, to be more exact, just three times – before coming back to generalise through my hat. And that doesn't count a day of green misery in a flat and grey place called Dungeness.

Time No. 1 was when I sat below a bell fixed by a clothes peg to the top of the heaviest and oldest pike rod I had. Those responsible for my indoctrination told me that all I had to do was wait and, when the bell rang, pull.

The main thing that I remember about that particular business was that when I hooked, or had my hook engulfed by, a starfish, it was like heaving up a coal bucket from the pit bottom.

The second time was when I spent a night on the pier – because they said that night was the best time. And the thing I remember about that is huddling, with an equally uninspired friend, over a primus. We tried to make cocoa while the sea mist slipped down our backs and only departed to make way for the cutting edge of the hardest wind in the world. The actual catch is something I don't remember.

During the day, pier anglers gossip in hearty fashion while waiting for the bells to ring. It was at such a time, when we all stood in shoulder-to-shoulder cluster along the rails, that someone told me that old yarn about Frank's ear.

Apparently the ear was torn off when the man at Frank's left side made an unusually energetic and uncontrolled cast, sending goodness knows how many pounds of lead and four hooks, off into infinity with one bloody lobe attached.

Sea anglers can produce the deepest of belly laughs. They did after this story. Maybe they always do after this story. Frank wasn't there when the tale was told to me, but as I have since heard that it was Jim or Harry or an angry Irishman on the east coast who lost the ear, it is obvious that someone did, somewhere, and will do so again tomorrow.

However, the incident which finally ended my brief and ham-fisted sea-fishing career was when a six foot six inch chap in a duffle coat first disposed of a barking conger with complete unconcern... and then got a bite which almost took him in on the end of his bucking rod.

'By Christ, it's something big!' he said, and everyone else on the breakwater left his bell and hurried up.

'Big', he growled again, puffing and bunching his shoulders and winching away.

That breakwater was so constructed that you couldn't see over it to the water immediately underneath. It sloped away in a baffling manner, so you just had to wait until your catch reached the top before identifying it.

Take it from me, the interest was strong as duffle coat strained and struggled, cursed and blew, everything creaking. Heave... and heave... and... 'It's coming up', he grunted. Heave...and heave and 'Stand BACK!'

We were all obeying the order to stand back (perhaps remembering the story of the ear) and so none of the onlookers could be the first to see what the big something was So the climax came in an unpleasant kind of way. Duffle coat froze. Then he threw away his rod. I'm telling you he did! He didn't say a word to us. Just grabbed his packet of cigarettes. Then he sort of staggered into a huddle with a close crony.

The best guess among the rest of us was that in another second an octopus would have come crawling over the parapet. One man was immediately inspired to launch another tale... about a shark-bitten human head he'd once seen.

That's enough for me. The sea is fine for looking at, sailing on and even for swimming in, if you don't mind

It Was Something Big! 131

the sailing boats, the oil and the toilet paper. And there's nothing better if you feel like a bit of windswept musing on being from a bold island race.

But I walked away from that last experience like a man who expects to be dragged in by tentacles at any moment, or step on a weever fish and be poisoned... or lose an ear.

26. Secret Stronghold

There's a place I don't often talk about. I call it mine, though it is rather less mine and rather more the Forestry Commission's. Only close angling friends are told about it (all two of them) and I curse my own selfishness in the matter, but it makes no difference.

A strip of old woodland lies beside open heath in front of my cottage. The heath is speckled with gorse, and some self-sown pines hold the middle distance. The wood is thick with trees and lies upon the heath like a bolster at the end of a wide mattress. And, hidden in coils around the heart of the wood, is a small stream which flows into a river. If the stream weren't hidden it wouldn't be mine – it would become everyone's and no-one's.

Outside the wood, the broader river is easily seen from the road. It is not worth fishing there. Sometimes it seems quiet and natural early in the morning or late in winter, but when the sun shines it takes the lid off a tin full of people.

They come out buzzing as bluebottles do, which is a sad thing to say, but they say they like being bluebottles because it makes them feel alive. They spill over the fields with many stoves, many folding deckchairs and many, many children. They bring inflatable dinghies to the river and, at a ford lower down, they wash their cars.

It takes only the smallest flicker of sun, the slightest sensation of warmth among the clouds, to set the road roaring continuously between cricket bats, bathing trunks and screams.

But in this bolster of woodland lying quiet by the heath,

the sun raises nothing but soft dust through the branches of oak and birch, hobo hollies and huge beeches which were pollarded in the days when cars were only a mad dream.

Why the place remains secret I don't know. Perhaps the river outside the wood acts as a decoy. Or it could be that the sagging fence, seen from the road, makes the wood look private and heavily keepered. It isn't, but I'm grateful for the illusion. Long may it play them false.

When I'm not away fishing seriously on waters everyone knows I come to the woodland stream merely to walk and stare. I can see its hiding place from the window of my workroom – so can my dog, who once fell in there when he was a tumble of puppy fat and a bit frightened of water.

The occasional picknicker sometimes dribbles in, voice gradually becoming hushed; the occasional pair of young lovers, carrying their own sunshine, float through. But most of the time the wood has only squirrels scratching edible ladders from the bark and the flutter of colour from jays who trail their coats all over the place.

I know that wagtails retreat here when they have grown tired of admiring themselves in the wing mirrors of visitors' cars. And that, one day, the village boys who work their way along the stream, creeping into the wood like muddied trolls, will kill the wagtails with their guns and catapults. They will kill with innocence, and true pride. They will exult as they did when they smashed the life from a kingfisher last season.

Yet I prefer the young killers, stalking or swaggering, to the transistorised crowds disgorged from the cities to dig up the primroses and put them into plastic wardrobe bags, or to sit, unknowing, over ice cream and paste sandwiches at the roadside river lido.

Behind them though, behind their backs, the stream in the wood runs silently. It flows in the manner of a partly unravelled birds nest of nylon line, twisting in trickles, doubling in a flurry of minor rapids and looping itself into impossible situations. Yet somehow it always comes back strongly on course.

At the merest hint of rain it bubbles, and at the first droplets it assaults the banks and strands of pebbles. Then, when the first heavy splashes come, it goes on guard against people.

As the rain falls, the stream comes tearing out of the wood, writhing like a hosepipe, and floods everything in sight. Once it flooded the high motor road, which made everyone swear, though it was a fine achievement, I thought, for a very small stream.

When the flood recedes, which it does rapidly, the true cunning of the stream's guard duty in the wood can be seen. It leaves a swamp just two footsteps inside the fence, so the visitors retreat. They don't know that a little further on is firm ground, leading to the water's edge.

For two years now I have been meaning to fish in this secret place, but for some reason I can't quite understand I have never done so. If ever a stream beckoned an angler, tugged at him, chattered invitingly inside his head, this one does.

You can hear the call as you watch it racing busily along in the spring, worrying into runnels which are nowhere deeper than ten inches, though sometimes it swirls in eddies where, rumour says, there's a depth of six feet, even at the low water of summer.

I suppose the reason why I haven't yet fished here (the Forestry Commission will let you for 25p a day, fly-only) is that this brave little stream is too idyllic. While I watch and walk and wonder, it might be the finest rough fishing in England. If I actually fish there, it might be revealed as barren and merely a pretty face.

In fact this is probably the case. After a lot of walking and watching I have seen nothing exciting. Once there was an eel and several times something of minnow quality dashed away. At a certain period of the year small jacks move along it to feast on mating frogs in adjacent bogland, but that's all.

Yet I started to wish for a rod in my hand when I met the forester just outside the wood. He was a wiry man who soon told me he didn't feel 75.

He leaned on a motorised saw (I wish it had been an axe) which had been in use all morning in service of the Forestry Commission who were worried about trees falling on campers in a spot where they were building a public lavatory. Then he told me that, next time I was around in the evening, he'd show me the big trout all right.

Since then, more evidence. A neighbour trapped me into an hour of home ciné films. I didn't think I'd be glad to be trapped and had visions of hours solid with concealed weariness before Aunt Ada's second wedding, or the holiday in Austria with many heroes in glory on the ski slopes.

Instead, the films were of natural history, and in one there was a dead trout. It was some trout, I can tell you. A lot between gills and vent had been ripped out – probably started by an otter and continued by crows – but it was a fish worth looking twice at.

Where had it been filmed? On the banks of the Wylye? The movie-maker showed me. He lifted a curtain and pointed out of his window. It had been found by the woodland stream.

A bit after that I met one of the village boys returning at dusk. There was a five-foot, bright-yellow glass rod over his shoulder, with a big green float rattling against it as he walked. In an old war-surplus gas-mask case he had four trout, and one looked as if it was nudging half a pound.

Despite a man-to-man promise that I wouldn't tell anybody about his not having a licence, he still wouldn't say much. Just shrivelled up into his shirt collar and looked foxy. But it was enough for me.

As the new trout season opens its doors I find I'm down for a few inches of the Test, a yard or two of the Itchen and some miles of the upper Avon. Should I let them take second place and try for some of those little wild ones in the secret stream?

Well it must be done soon, and quickly. There are rumours that the Forestry Commission are thinking of making the wood into a 'riverside park'. And even if they don't there's always the fear that visiting hordes down by the road might move into the wood and discover the stream for themselves. It has happened everywhere else...

27. Long-Lost Christmas

Evocative. That's the word I want. Evocative. In dictionary language it means calling up memories, feelings and energies. In my language it means a piece of card with rough parchment edges measuring seven inches by five.

It is a Christmas card. Or rather, it was a Christmas card, once. I bought it to send to a fishing friend of long standing; one of those rare and valuable fellows who do not change with the years. Perhaps he wasn't so valuable though, or else I should have posted the card. Instead, he got a Father Christmas climbing down a chimney. A fat Father Christmas, and a very small chimney. It was the sort of card that comes from bumper gift packs, and I half suspect that I left the pencilled price on the back... 2d.

But the fine, large, evocative card I had to keep for myself. The picture on it calls up feelings and energies, certainly, but not, I am sad to say, memories. My experience doesn't stretch so far.

Here is the interior of an inn, an old wood-panelled inn, painted with all the shades of Autumn. It is warm and brown and red. The anglers wear leggings or chimney-pipe trousers. Their hats are tall and their faces are flushed with inner delight and the frosty air over the river, which can just be seen running outside the inn door. The landlord, fat and aproned, and ruddy with a trencherman's good fellowship, is standing by, with big fists full of big tankards. Around the mellowed room are heavy tables, and you can almost feel the oak. The anglers seated there are winding on floats, playing with winches and obviously talking of happy fishy things over a clutter of creels and nets.

Long-Lost Christmas

A touch of age and dust is over the colours now, but the fishermen are still alive and happy. I have never seen fishermen like them. I never will. Logically, they must still be around, in modern dress, but, because I am dressed in the same fashion, I shan't find them.

In a way this old card represents an ideal dream. Foolishly, I have always had in mind the desire to discover that scene for myself; to walk through the next inn door I come to, and see...

It is the same sort of ideal dream that comes to you in idle moments when you wonder what you'd do if you won thousands of pounds. You don't expect to win thousands of pounds on the pools (nor do you expect to work for them), but it's a compelling little game all the same.

Maybe the card-that-was-never-sent had something to do with it, but for a long time now I have always had the desire to go fishing, just for an hour or so, on Christmas Day mornings. This is unlike the ordinary feeling you get when you think of going fishing. This is a special evocative feeling. Christmas is special; catching fish is special – put the two together and you have a unique delight.

I'm saying nothing about the family problems of Christmas Day fishing, except to deliver it as my considered opinion that any angler who cannot get out of his obligations deserves all he gets. No, I'm not underestimating the difficulties. And yes, I don't always succeed either.

Obviously on the Christmas Day for which I bought the card there was a pressing need to go fishing. One look at those old anglers and their Christmas was enough to make me pack my tackle in the car, alongside the holly and the presents.

This Christmas was being spent away from home with people who lived miles from any river. How such nice-to-be-with folk could be found in such an arid place is something that has always puzzled me. Still, they had The Ponds.

Not an angler's agony of delight, The Ponds. Not the sort of place that appears on anglers' cards. But good enough when you are itching to fish and Christmas morn is hard and bright.

I felt then, as I have since in other places, the particular pleasure just setting off for a spot of Christmas fishing brings. It came as I passed by suburban houses with the cold metropolitan pavements ringing so sharply that they seemed about to crack. Past the church, surrounded by parked cars of the dutiful and the grateful. Past the odd lonely walker who gave a sideways glance of surprise at a man with fishing rods, before sliding back to the warmth of turkey to come, and from which he had only emerged to let his dog use a lamp-post.

Soon the houses and bus stops gave way to common land and silver birches, then there were ditches instead of pavements and everything held in frosty silence edged with traces of the snow, which, of course, had come too early and hadn't really stayed.

Then I was at The Ponds with my breath hanging in the air and blood warmed by the walk. Normally these waters are hidden under the rods of many anglers, the muslin nets of even more small boys, and whole fleets of model boats, bathers, ice-cream packets and carelessly-hit tennis balls.

Now it was deserted, locked quietly and almost beautifully in a coffin of ice. The ice extended from all banks, and closed in like segments of a camera aperture, not quite meeting but leaving a hole in the middle.

I fished for pike. It was the only thing to do, and the only thing I wanted to do. I used a shallow diving plug that looked like an ornament from the Christmas tree – bright, yet somehow not garish; gay, yet not quite trivial.

As the long cast was made to the distant area of clear water in the middle of one of the ponds, the plug flashed under its new coating of frost. Then the faint far-off plop as it landed in the water. Satisfying.

It was Christmas fishing as anglers of any period in English history would understand it. The line drooping across the expanse of ice, throwing up frosted and powdered spray as the plug was worked, and then the glinting thing lolloping back on the reel-in, its hooks hissing.

I cast for an hour and a half of this stolen time. At midday the sound of church-bells came to the ponds. A swan waddled over the ice and flourished his wings. He moved near my line as I juggled it, and at first I thought the sudden heavy jerk was caused by his beating wings. But then the rod gave a vicious nod and the jerk became a pull. I brought the rod back in a long sweep over my shoulder, and 20 yards away there was a rolling splash.

The line began to whine. I felt like shouting for the fun of it as, for a second, I had a picture in my mind of a great, flopping, Christmas pike toboganning over the ice to the gaff I had ready.

It was not to be. Somewhere out in the middle the pike made a long dive for it and hauled trace and line under the ice. The monofil cut in as wire cuts cheese. Then everything stopped. Suddenly. An insecurely hooked treble came away and the bright yellow and red plug bobbed up.

Yet the loss was no loss. It left no dead feeling inside. Christmas fishing is pleasure of itself. So it wasn't my failure that made me feel just a small twinge of disappointment.

There was no oak-panelled inn to visit on the way back, and I did feel rather like striding in to one. I wanted to call heartily for a steaming posset, throw my rod on a heavy table, and gather around me cheery anglers to hear the tale of a Christmas pike that had got away. But that was a momentary fancy. I was later content with a modern sherry. And I thought not a harsh thing of all the suburban men in their houses, lying fat under paper hats, anglers among them.

Of all the Christmases that have passed since then I remember only a few. Once, when I was without rods, there was a small boy who thought fishing on the great day was fun too. We went to a river, with makeshift tackle, and I caught him a roach with fins as red as Santa Claus's robe.

The fish was taken legering, with a butterfly nut from the boy's cycle as a weight. He thought I was some sort of genius. He doesn't think that now. For I have grown fat under paper hats myself, these days, and the years spring forward, leaving a jumble behind. The card from the past is still before me each Christmas, though many times it has almost been thrown away.

One day maybe, when the last frost lies on the water and the fire splutters for the last time, the landlord will have an extra tankard in his hands and my rods will be beside theirs on those massive tables.

I'll tell them, then, about the monster pike that lived in a fine lake and fought me for hours one Christmas in an age that they do not know . . .

28. Last Cast

Whatever it looks like, this isn't a book about the end of the world. Neither is it about the Massachusetts Institute of Technology. For one thing, I am told that the Americans don't go fishing, they go hunting fish. And, for another thing, those of us who suspect that the sport is doomed, go fishing in order to forget about it.

We even manage to laugh over our sandwich boards, but our laughter has an echo which is shrill. Angling is now known to have more participants than any other sport in Britain, so perhaps it is safer that most of them do not believe in that fashionable word 'eco-catastrophe'.

The Massachusetts Institute of Technology found out about the end of the world by feeding its computers with all the statistics. Without even an apologetic pause, the computer backed all the distracted scientists and gave us something less than the end of the century for Doomsday. And, on the whole, the 1972 U.N. Conference at Stockholm was hardly more encouraging.

Those scientists are striding around the street corners warning about overpopulation, pollution, water abstraction, declining natural resources, failing green revolutions and the death of the topsoil. Some of us who listened wished we hadn't, so we just went fishing rather more often than before.

But the computer was asked another question: 'How can we prevent the end of the world?' And its short answer was – 'you can't'.

All of this happy information won't help you catch bigger fish, but it will confirm the general dislike of computers. And if the four horsemen really are saddling-up, then it should make you try a bit harder for that 2 lb. roach.

It does seem, though, that those anglers who are starting now have quite a problem. I'm a little put out because I've only been fishing seriously for 25 years and that's about half the time necessary to learn a quarter of all there is to know about the drug we call angling. However, the new chaps, young or old, who have just bought their first rod (something nasty and efficient in glass, almost certainly) and their first fixed spool reel (centrepin, what's that?) might just get twenty years in, according to the more optimistic apostles of doom – but prospects will be declining all the way.

One distinguished angling club, which is almost Masonic in its approach to potential new members, appears to be aware of the trend. A chap told me about them when I was throwing things at trout in the Test. As the trout didn't seem interested I got yakking instead.

Together we stared at the clear chalk flow and this chap said that this club was digging holes all over the country.

'Working on a twenty year plan' he said, with a kind of satisfaction. 'They reckon that in twenty years there'll be hardly any fishable rivers left'.

Now that's foresight for you! The future has a rainbow at the end of it... indeed, dozens of rainbows in holes in the ground. And in twenty years, when the last gallon from the great rivers has been flushed down the lavatory pans, we'll at least have our put-and-take trout fisheries.

Shall we buy tickets and approach these new waters through turnstiles? Or must we put our sons' names down now and save hard for the fees? Consult your brokers, those who haven't been invited to join farsighted clubs, and get some advice. Should we send our kids to Eton or budget for a season or two at the lake in A.D. 2000?

It's a brave man who says all this won't happen. It's a brave man who tells MIT that it's talking nonsense and everything is going to be all right. I haven't met such a person yet, but I'm still searching. This is one subject on which we all want to be proved wrong.

For the time being it would be good to believe that

today's new anglers will know simplicity and true ease. Yet these qualities seem gone from the art. Indeed, they have been slipping away for years, and the process is now accelerating.

Great experts tell me that more fish and bigger fish are being caught now than in the past, but that's because there are more people fishing more frantically and with more information at their command. Any old angler will tell the newcomer that the overall quality of fishing has declined. Mind you, old anglers have been saying that for centuries past, but it had to come true some day. And if you don't believe wrinkled ancients, then you can always ask the computer... the answer will be the same.

In order to catch educated, twice-caught fish from sickly waters while shoulder to shoulder with his fellow contemplative men, the new angler should take his degree in piscatology.

This involves a scientific study that goes far beyond the old demands which were to do with hook, line and bait. Now we must know about swing tips and quiver tips, spring indicators and swim feeders, block feeders and soluble plastic, hypodermic syringes for worms... and that's only half the list. As for floats – the essential knowledge here comes only after deep research.

Under these pressures, anglers are changing. Of course it is still wise to know about being quiet and being observant in a natural way. But the modern angler, which is what the beginner wants to be, is becoming a craftsman on piece rates.

I think we go fishing because it's the last old freedom to seem easily come by, yet the modern angling scene puts tension on the rod tip where once a dragonfly rested.

The boy is never seen with mythical stick and bent pin. Now he comes to the water loaded like his dad with a kind of portable workshop filled with many new devices. It is the same for me, and you, and him over there.

Pressure is on, even for those who don't know about the end of the world. Let's not go fishing for fun, but for a bit of peace or for the illusion of the last wilderness. How long can the boy's sense of wonder last? Sadly, perhaps not much beyond boyhood.

You get up early to go fishing, says the tradition. But now, in most places, you get up early in order to get some fishing. If you don't, the other chap's umbrella, his green-roofed workshop, will be there before you – keeping the rain off and the fish off too.

And the trout must all come out as soon as they are put in, and the dace are without top lips, and where have the roach gone asks an angling newspaper. Where have the perch gone, asks another. And the salmon have ulcers and the cod have DDTs, except those in certain places which have arsenic instead, or mercury.

Well, let's grab it all while we can, there are still places which can offer what our fathers knew. Fish on, fish hard and no more alarmist talk, you say? Sure, man, sure!

My fishing book doesn't mention computers, or offer the latest gadget for beating your neighbour out of doors. But I do hope that it sketches something of the fading scene and the fading sensations, without being too serious.